POTTERY
A Manual of Techniques

Doug Wensley

The Crowood Press

First published in 1989 by
The Crowood Press Ltd
Ramsbury, Marlborough
Wiltshire SN8 2HR

Paperback edition 1992

This impression 1996

British Library Cataloguing-in-Publication Data

A catalogue record for this book is available from the British Library

ISBN 1 85223 717 1

All black and white photographs by the author and Judith Wensley, except page 46 R. J. Whittick
FRPS, pages 47 and 50 Cromartie Kilns Ltd.
Line-drawings by Sharon Perks.

To William Ruscoe, Rosie and John

Typeset by Acorn Bookwork, Salisbury, Wiltshire
Printed in Great Britain by The Bath Press

Contents

Acknowledgements

To Judith Wensley, whose expert comments and suggestions have been invaluable, as have her assistance and demonstration for the photographs. Her patience and the insights she offered while typing the manuscript have also contributed significantly and have been much appreciated.

I am also grateful for the help offered by Steve Abbott and Peter Dworak, Rufford Craft Centre, Nottinghamshire, and for the use of colour transparencies by Nic Broomhead from their library.

Thanks to Cromartie Kilns Ltd who have been generous with photographs and encouragement.

For the use of their slides and photographs, thanks to Jane Hamlin, Phil Jolley, John Leach, Janet Lewis, Martin Lewis, John Pollex, Dave Roberts, William Ruscoe, Josie Walter, and John Wheeldon.

Thanks also to the numerous craftspeople whose friendship and professional support have been generously given over the years.

Introduction

Clay has been used by human beings for many hundreds of years. Evidence discovered deep underground in caves at Tuc d'Audoubert, in the Ariege area of France, indicates that palaeolithic mankind modelled with the medium to produce ritualistic sculptures some 20,000 years ago. From that time clay has been used extensively in wide-ranging manifestations of human creativity and self-expression.

The material we know as clay has always been freely available. It was soon discovered that clay could readily be modelled into forms which, when dried, became semi-permanent. Although most people today consider clay to be synonymous with the art of pottery, it is perhaps worth remarking that whereas clay has been generally used for a very long time, possibly in excess of 50,000 years, its use for specifically pot-making purposes is rather less ancient. There is no evidence of its use for pottery until about 6,000 BC, at which time pots were being made in clay in Asia Minor, Syria and Anatolia.

From that location and period there developed a craft activity based on the 'ceramic' process. Artefacts both ritualistic and utilitarian were made in clay (*earth*) made plastic by *water* content, and transformed into a new material by the action of heat (*fire*). This trinity of earth, fire and water has been recognised for many hundreds of years.

Some anonymous early peoples perhaps noticed that clay remained plastic if left in the damp, cool atmosphere of a cave; on the other hand, if clay artefacts were exposed to the drier atmosphere of wind and sun, they dried out and maybe broke in the process. It would further have been noticed that in this dry state such objects were rather fragile. Probably by accident, possibly by design, and at very different places and times, artefacts must have been subjected to the action of fire. It may have been, also, that crude vessels were fashioned to contain and store foodstuffs such as nuts, berries, or even liquids. In the latter case it would have been noticed that the vessels would gradually collapse, disintegrating as they became saturated.

At some point the critical observation would have been made that when clay was heated thoroughly in a fire, a significant change took place. It would have been noticed that when the clay was allowed to cool it would no longer disintegrate if it came into contact with water. An irreversible transformation had taken place after which it was no longer possible to reclaim the clay. Even if ground into dust it could not be reconstituted into its original state of plasticity. The new material could not be broken down by the addition of water, neither was it fragile. In fact, it had become durable and, as a result, much more useful. Nevertheless it would still be porous – a property which offered advantages as well as disadvantages.

It may have been that people

accidentally 'burned' or 'fired' vessels which had been specifically fashioned for storage purposes. At different times and places other accidents may have occurred which led to the gradual realisation of ceramics as a concept. Whenever and wherever the ceramic process was discovered, a technological revolution was achieved. The concept of ceramics would have emerged, been developed, spread out to other peoples, and would be quickly refined to suit the needs of the societies it came to serve.

Perhaps you will allow me to pursue a little further this idiosyncratic overview of the development of the craft. By doing so you will perhaps understand how we have arrived at the sophisticated ceramics technology of the present day. At a time when this technology has been applied to space exploration, it is still also used in a slightly less prosaic way to produce simple hand-crafted pots. In fact, one of the most appealing aspects of the studio potter's craft to many people is its almost ageless tradition, using simple materials and procedures which have evolved or been developed over long periods of time. Underlying any novel avant-garde method of manipulating clay, for example, there is usually a simple 'caveman' principle at work. Much the same could be said of other ceramic processes, such as decoration, glazing or firing. So let us return briefly to what I tend to call the 'original situation'.

The caves in which palaeolithic man lived were relatively young when compared to the great age of the surrounding rocks and clay. Nevertheless they were utilised by early man who often competed with animals for the protection caves could afford against changing climatic conditions and unwelcome pred-

atory visitors. Inhabitants of caves would have often found them part-filled with clay and other debris washed in over great periods of time. It is more than possible that pebbles could be found partially embedded in the surface of such deposits which formed conveniently uniform floors in an otherwise dark chaos of rock and water.

Having removed such a water-worn rock or pebble either to explore the indentation, or to make a sleeping space more comfortable, it would not have been long before someone familiar with 'ceramics' used the depression as a mould to make a clay vessel. By pressing a thin slab of plastic clay into the hole, a dish could be made which would shrink as it dried. The action of shrinking would release the dish from the walls of the mould, and with care it could then be removed. After sufficient drying it could be subjected to the rigours of the fire, rendering it suitable for storing or consuming liquids or solids. If damaged or broken, or when it became rancid due to its porosity, the dish could easily be replaced.

The implications of this technology must have been enormous. Modelled objects, both utilitarian and ritualistic, could be transformed by fire from the original, humble earth-and-water clay into a new, virtually indestructible material – ceramic. Societies would possibly, as a result, have taken on new ideological and philosophical ideas relating to trial or purification by fire. Whatever else may have happened as a result of this particular enlightenment, we can be sure that human inventiveness would have been applied to other areas of potential development. More satisfying and more practical methods of production would

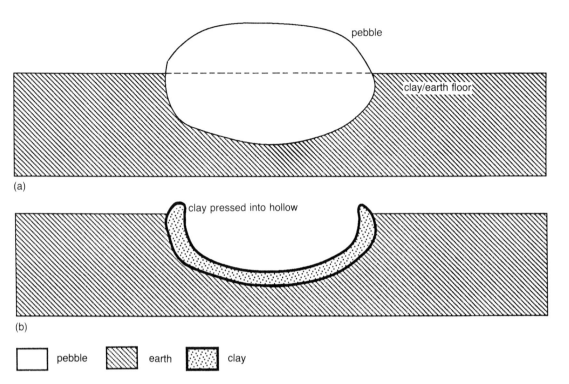

(a)

(b)

pebble   earth   clay

(a) Water-worn pebble partly embedded in cave floor. (b) If the pebble is removed, the resulting dish-shaped indentation could be used as a simple storage place, or as a mould into which a clay slab is pressed to form a dish, which could then be carried about and duplicated as required.

then have been conceived, while it would have been possible to observe more clearly the problems of firing wares, and to experiment with techniques designed to solve or avoid them.

Working simultaneously in different parts of the world there are potters who have only partly been able to overcome some of these difficulties, and others who enjoy, if that is the appropriate word, the advantages of high technology. Peasant potters, for instance, who bonfire vessels using dried grasses or dung as fuel have to offset losses resulting from uneven distribution of heat. They are obliged to make very many more pots than are actually required, to allow for the high percentage of cracked wares. Such potters have to adopt a philosophical attitude to the inevitable accidental losses incurred in their firing process. Alternatively, they must attempt, with whatever local resources are available, to overcome the basic problem by designing a more efficient means of firing. In a modern industrial pottery such losses are minimised by careful regulation of clay bodies, methods of production, and sophisticated firing procedures which are contrived to provide predictable outcomes with maximum economy of labour, materials and fuel.

Contemporary studio pottery, hand-made by artist-craftpersons using traditional, time-honoured and tested methods, encounters both the pitfalls, the problems and the delights inherent in the primitive approach to the craft. At the same time it embraces some of the advantages of modern technology which may be considered appropriate to the specific needs of a workshop or classroom. There is no merit in either putting work at risk in the interests of a misguided 'back-to-nature' acceptance of the crude or inept, nor in wasting valuable resources such as materials, time or fuel, all of which are irreplaceable.

At this point I have returned to the basic reason for writing this book. The combination of an awareness of the extensive historic evidence of mankind's use of clay, and of practical difficulties, if not downright mysticism and alchemy, is often somewhat intimidating. Any aspiring potter is inevitably influenced by the consequences of a craft evolved over such an impressive period of time and by the variety of requirements imposed by the societies which have produced it. Probably one of the most potent images a beginner has to come to terms with is that of the potter working at a wheel. It is as compelling as it can be off-putting to see such skilful dexterity demonstrated as to suggest magical control over an inanimate material. To some observers the process appears almost illusory. Perhaps it is reassuring, then, to attempt to site the wheel chronologically. Against the geological timescale of the millions of years necessary for feldspathic rock to be eroded and rotted down into the raw material we know as clay, the development of such a piece of technology as the potter's wheel is very recent. Even when viewed in relation to the other known usages of clay, the wheel can be seen to have emerged comparatively recently. It was developed in the Middle East, somewhere in the third millennium before Christ. Pottery is not necessarily synonymous with the wheel. In fact it was another two thousand years or so before Western European potters became acquainted with it.

Many peasant and artist potters, contemporary and from ancient civilisations, have produced delicate or monumental artefacts without recourse to the wheel. They have exploited the properties of the medium in many and varied ways, producing fragile porcelain pots and models, or massive projects such as the recently discovered life-sized Chinese warriors. Anyone with a love of clay, a feeling for it, and an understanding of the basic processes can produce exciting, fulfilling ceramic artefacts. The challenge to produce wares on a wheel may well be there – you may feel that that is what you really want to do. However, in the event of your not having the interest in the wheel, the necessary skills, or the time to acquire them, or even the necessary wheel itself, do not feel that you are at a disadvantage, lacking or inadequate as a potential potter. It might be reassuring to remember that virtually all industrially produced pottery is made *without* the use of a wheel.

The tactile qualities of clay can be experienced and enjoyed, ceramic work produced, and the fascinating processes of decoration and firing all be carried out in a shed and backyard, or at an evening class. Whether you have started potting at school, at a local college, or at home, I hope this book will assist and encourage you to pursue your interest to the full, and give you the confidence to attempt a wider range of ceramic activity. It is certainly my intention to remove some of the mysticism from firing kilns in particular, so that anyone responsible for infrequent firing of school kilns, for example, will be better equipped to manage successfully both the contents and the kiln.

1 What is Clay?

It is difficult for children or adults not to respond to clay in an imaginative and creative way. The material begs to be used. It invites manipulation and defies the logic of clean hands, clothes and kitchen work surfaces. It prompts us to use it and explore its possibilities, and we feel the need somehow to transform the humble material into something more enduring. We poke it, squeeze it, pat it and manipulate it with our hands and fingers. We attach appendages on to our newly created artefact. We smooth it, pinching and coaxing until we are satisfied with the result. We find that the material develops too many cracks to be acceptable – we realise that we have handled the material too long in warm, dry hands, and we return the clay to the river bed or plastic bag and start again. After all, its only mud . . .

Or is it? The simplicity of the material is deceptive. Mud does not have great potential, as many young children have discovered. A mixture of sand and water is no substitute either, however fine the sand might be. So what is clay, and what is it that makes it so special? The answer to the first part of the question is easy; it is rotten rock.

Over millions of years igneous rocks decompose, producing the unique material we recognise as clay. Dartmoor provides a graphic, if simplified, example, the decomposed material compressed between a granite cap above and other rock below. It is quarried at various places around the lower edges of the moor, where it is, or can be, exposed such as near Kingsteignton in the River Teign valley, South Devon. It almost seems to ooze out from beneath the huge granite cap of the moor, providing a valuable source of Devon ball clay.

Clays found at their places of origin, are known as primary clays. Clays dug from beds deposited by the action of glaciers or rivers, which are carried from the

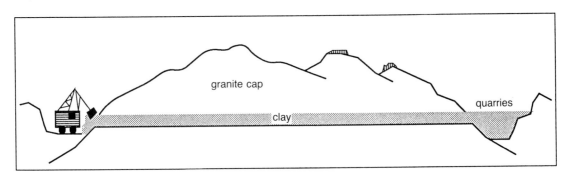

Dartmoor. Rotted feldspathic rock becomes clay. Under pressure it seems to ooze out from under the moor to be quarried, as at Bovey Tracey.

primary site and finally dumped else-where, are known as secondary.

Clays from different sources vary in colour and composition, and some have different properties, some being more plastic than others. Impurities in the clay, too, give rise to variations in drying and firing characteristics.

So what *is* it that makes clay such an attractive material, capable of being used in so many ways? It is a unique material in that, as already mentioned, it is usu-ally plastic. It can be pinched, rolled, thrown, cast or spun into almost any shape; it can be extruded, stamped, pierced or scored when used in its soft, moistened state. When allowed to dry it can be broken down, re-moistened, and used for making something else. Apart from its variety of colour or texture (which can vary from an exceedingly smooth fine body to an extremely gritty, coarse one), the most obvious property is its unique plasticity when moist. A major reason for this plasticity is the incredibly small size of clay particles, which can be thought of as minute single crystals. An electron microscope is necessary to see the particle size of these crystals; there is often in excess of three and a half million of them in one cubic millimetre of a fine-grained clay body such as ball clay. In addition, each grain is shaped rather like a discus, so that when lubricated with water (each minute particle wetted on all its surface area), and arranged so that all or most of the grains are lying in a similar plane, the material achieves its maximum plasticity – some bodies are found to be more plastic than others.

The increase in popularity of the craft of pottery in educational establishments, hobby potter workshops, and with pro-fessional potters, has in turn caused a growth in the demand for readily avail-able, reliable supplies of suitable clays. Very few potters actually quarry their own; the range of commercially pro-duced bodies is probably broad enough to satisfy even the most demanding of requirements. My intention here, there-fore, is not so much to provide technical pointers to blending one's own clay body, but simply to indicate the range of choice available from conventional sources. I am sure that most of us, at least at the start of our ceramic activities, will be able to purchase, ready prepared, a clay body more than capable of fulfill-ing our needs. It is with this in mind that I will only briefly describe clays which would not normally be used on their

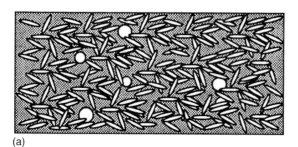

(a)

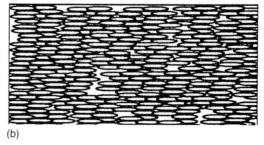

(b)

Particle arrangements. (a) Disc-shaped clay particles haphazardly scattered throughout the clay reduce plasticity, causing it to appear 'short'. (b) When particles are arranged in the same plane the body becomes more plastic. Discs are lubricated with water and so slide easily one against the other.

own, and treat in broad terms those in general use.

If you are fortunate enough to have a free supply of natural clay at the bottom of your garden, you will naturally want to make use of it if at all possible. It would be most satisfying to know that even the most basic process of mining the clay had been controlled by yourself, and would in addition add a unique quality to the wares produced.

One basic fact about clay is that it is incredibly common. It is one of the earth's natural resources, readily available in one form or another almost everywhere, is usually easy to find and acquire, and is therefore relatively cheap. Clay has been found all over the world, and there can be few societies which have been unable to make use of local deposits. Where it is not readily available, however, it is likely to be expensive, not only because of its scarcity, but also due to its weight and bulk, neither of which make it cheap to transport.

Probably the most familiar clay is a red-brown colour, often referred to as terracotta ('brown earth'), and this has been used universally for the production of plant pots, chimney pots and ridge tiles, not to mention bricks and drainpipes. Table ware will usually be at least partially glazed, as seen in the traditional North Devon milk and harvest jugs. Being a secondary clay, this type is usually very plastic and can sometimes be used straight from the ground without any problems of major impurity being encountered. In addition to its major ingredient, clay, it also contains red iron oxide as an impurity. This provides the body with its characteristic warm colour and gives rise to its 'red earth' title. Other secondary clays, which vary in colour

from warm buff to blue-grey, contain less iron oxide, but possibly contain traces of other less common oxides such as manganese. Some also contain vegetable particles and stains which will burn away in the fire, reducing the colour range to a toasted biscuit colour. This colour will vary according to the source and exact type of clay.

Most clays, when fired, will retain some degree of colour. This will be heightened if covered with a transparent glaze. In this manner a light biscuit colour will perhaps become rather more yellow and slightly darker in tone. Red earthenware, when transparently glazed, will appear mahogany brown. A pure white body, or clay, is not easy to find naturally, probably due mainly to the fact that theoretically 'pure' clay (kaolin) is likely to have become contaminated by other minerals over the very long time it has taken to become clay. If it has later been washed out or carried around by river or glacier and deposited elsewhere, the likelihood of contamination will have been increased. One of the world's rare sources of pure kaolin is in Cornwall. Huge spoil heaps from clay works are a familiar sight, particularly on the southern edges of Bodmin Moor, and in wet weather local streams run milky white as the pure china clay is washed away by the rainwater. This true clay contains only silica, alumina and water, the latter being driven off by heat, as will be discussed in a little more detail later.

As a general rule, sources of naturally occurring clay, either primary or secondary, are not really of much practical interest to the craft potter, because these clays will have characteristics which make them unsuitable for immediate use. China clay, although wonderfully white, is not plastic; ball clay is rather too 'sticky' to be used on its own. Other clays contain a miscellany of foreign bodies which, for one reason or another, render the clay unuseable. They often require washing, sieving, and perhaps blending with other clays to produce an acceptable medium. Most potters, understandably, shy away from such procedures, which on a small scale are extremely time consuming and are physically hard work. An instantly available, usable body would not, in any event, be achieved, as clays require a period of time to 'mature'. Fortunately a wide range of prepared bodies can be purchased from pottery suppliers, some of whom are listed in the back of the book under Useful Addresses (page 190). Consult their catalogues and check with their technical advisors. Talk to other potters in your area. Both potters and suppliers are ready to advise, and may also let you have samples to try prior to making a choice.

The characteristics required of a particular body will depend on several factors. First there may be some preference for colour, possibly based on subsequent firing or decoration requirements. Second, the means by which the ware is produced will need to be considered. A smooth body with excellent throwing qualities may not be so suitable for building large-scale, slab-built sculptural pieces.

Let us return to the concept of pure 'mother' clay. A fine-grained body such as ball clay will consist exclusively of clay particles. Some clays, as dug, are relatively pure, but contain a measure of fine silica or sand particles in addition to the clay. Others, such as fire clay, contain coarser granules of silica and other refractory material, and are significantly less plastic than ball clay. The 'impure' content of silica granules is actually very important in several respects. As has already been mentioned, clay shrinks as it dries and when it is fired. Any refractory material (that which has already been subjected to heat), be it sand or ground up pottery, has already shrunk, and will therefore reduce the overall shrinkage of a clay body to which it is added. A thirty per cent addition of silica to ball clay will reduce overall shrinkage from, say, twelve per cent to eight per cent. It will also stiffen the body, providing a 'skeleton' for the 'muscle'. Thirdly, being refractory, it will not be affected by the heat of the kiln, reducing shrinkage, and increasing resistance to thermal shock, warping, splitting or dunting.

It might be tempting at this stage to make a decision as to the type of clay body required, based on the above. You might decide that a terracotta colour would be pleasant; but as the clay will be required for large-scale modelling it should contain a moderately coarse 'grog' to give it the necessary stiffness. It will also be used for oven-to-table ware, so it will also need a built-in tolerance of thermal shock. Such a broadly based brief is not unreasonable, but it has to be seen against a proposed maximum temperature when the body is eventually fired in the kiln. It might, however, be prudent to wait to discover how this final stage in the ceramic process affects clay bodies, glazes and cost. It can also to some extent determine the form of the proposed objects. A final decision can then be made as to the ideal clay body for your use.

Initial contact with pottery is usually via school, or part-time evening classes. In such an institutional setting, choice of clay and type of ware produced may well have been made for you. In the interests of efficiency and economy the workshop will be geared to earthenware or stoneware, and students may even be unaware that an alternative exists, if only in theory. So what exactly do the terms 'earthenware' and 'stoneware' mean? When completely dried out, clay still contains water in its molecular structure; Al_2O_3 (alumina) + $2SiO_2$ (silica) + $2H_2O$ (water). Only the 'free'' water has disappeared. By adding free water again the clay can be reclaimed (returned to its moist, plastic state). If, however, the dried clay is subjected to heat in excess of about 350°C, an irreversible change takes place whereby water within the molecular structure of the clay is driven off, changing the body forever. The clay can no longer be recycled by the addition of water – it becomes a totally new material.

At 350°C the new material is fragile and requires much higher temperatures in order to become hard enough for safe handling. However, if heated to 900–1,000°C it will have become hard and porous, and can be considered 'earthenware'. If the body is fired to higher temperatures, a second metamorphosis takes place. From 1,100°C upwards to 1,300°C most clay bodies will begin to melt, fusing particles together, vitrifying the body so that it becomes impervious to moisture. At this second stage the ware is considered to be 'stoneware'. These definitions will be returned to when discussing firing and glazing, but it is perhaps sufficient here to make the basic distinction and to indicate a very significant relationship between body, firing temperature, and potential effects upon the fired body of impurities contained in it.

2 Preparation

When a clay body has been identified and purchased it will arrive wrapped and treated ready for immediate use. It will probably have been weighed out in convenient lumps of fifty-six pounds (25.5kg) and pre-packaged in polythene bags, usually kept closed by a wire fastening at the throat of the bag. Such bags are best stored in a cool place until required, and will keep very well if wrapped overall in more polythene, stacked in a bin or dustbin, and should be protected from heat. Although these bags appear waterproof, the contents can in fact dry out even if the bags are not opened or damaged, so it is probably best not to purchase more than can properly be stored to prevent this happening. Most of us have a bag or two of hardened clay we must get around to reclaiming 'some time'. Unfortunately there are usually more interesting things to do with our time and the bags just sit there waiting. So prevention, as usual, is better than a cure.

Having opened a first bag of clay and made a start on the production of wares, it is inevitable that a considerable amount of the precious material will not actually find its way into the kiln. Disasters, false starts, turnings, scrapings and slurry from the wheel mount up and will require attention. Opened bags will require resealing and preferably securing in an airtight bin, possibly with the addition of damp cloths to prevent drying. A system will therefore be required to keep every-

thing in hand. To set up such a system it is necessary to know and understand what exactly you are attempting to achieve. That at least is pretty straightforward. In order to use clay easily it should be plastic, moist and easy to mould. It should be homogeneous, that is to say completely even in consistency, with no denser or soggy pockets within the mass, and containing no air bubbles, pockets of free water, or foreign bodies which could either damage walls of pots in the making, or burn away in the firing. To these ends it is probably best to keep dry clay away from plastic; break lumps (dry or leather-hard) down into reasonably small pieces prior to soaking down, and provide covered containers to prevent contamination by dust, debris or inappropriately allocated materials. It has been my experience that an open bin of 'soak' attracts all manner of rubbish. People will deposit crisp bags, cigarette ends or waste paper in what is obviously not a waste bin, whether they be visitors to a studio pottery, or students in a college.

RECLAIM

Ideally, damp clay should be kept damp after use so that it can be mixed up (kneaded or wedged) and restored ready for use. Clay which is too stiff for immediate recycle should be allowed to dry out completely, broken up into small pieces and soaked down in water to be recycled later. This is the technique to adopt with dried out bags of clay too. If a large lump of clay is hard but still damp it will be extremely difficult to break up, and because moist clay tends to be impervious to moisture (a fact which results in inadequate drainage where clay lies under the surface of a garden or field), it will also not soak down readily when water is added. Completely dry clay, on the other hand, will, if broken down into small pieces, take up water quite quickly. In fact it does not actually absorb the water. The water causes the particles of clay to separate and break down so that as the clay settles out it has the feel and texture of an 'open' granular slurry.

Having been broken down and put to soak in a suitable container, the dry clay will slake down and settle, and surface water will clear. The level of the clay will sink and the depth of surface water will increase until no further change is noticed. The water can now be decanted off and the clay allowed to dry out prior to wedging and kneading.

If left in its container the clay will dry unevenly, probably developing a hard, dry crust on the surface whilst still remaining too wet at the bottom. To prevent this the clay should be removed from the bin and spread out so that a maximum surface is exposed to the air. If possible the slops should be dumped out

Reclaimed clay, soaked down, spread out on a plaster slab to stiffen.

on an absorbent surface, such as a plaster of Paris slab so that drying can take place from below as well as above. Try to avoid nonporous surfaces, such as formica, in any case; the clay adheres to it and can be very difficult to remove. Unpainted wooden surfaces are useful, as are concrete paving slabs.

When the clay is initially removed from the bin it will probably be very wet and will tend to spread somewhat. But as it stiffens a little it is possible to speed up the process of drying by adopting the 'horseshoe' technique. The only piece of equipment needed is a plank. A length of scaffolding plank is ideal.

Using both hands make rough sausages of clay about a foot (60cm) long and about two or three inches (5–15cm) in circumference. There is no need for exact symmetry; the aim is simply to present as large a surface area as possible to the air. Arrange the sausages in inverted horseshoe arches along the board in a line so that air can circulate around the exposed surfaces.

If regular checks are made on its progress it will soon be possible to knock the loops of clay together ready for the next

stage of its preparation. The question is often asked, 'How long will it take for clay or a pot to dry out?' Obviously that depends on weather, atmosphere in the preparation area, and how thick the clay might be. Surfaces will dry before the inner mass of clay so care has to be exercised in controlling the stiffening on the outside. Hard, dry corners or edges should be prevented, and it might be advisable to re-roll the sausages from time to time, exposing new wet surfaces. Very thin loops of clay could dry out very quickly, especially in a well-ventilated situation so they would need frequent inspection, probably every few minutes rather than every few hours. Use whatever method is appropriate at the time.

A small quantity of reclaim can be dumped out in a press dish mould to start with; large quantities could be dumped directly on to any clean surface, be it floor or strong bench top. Depending upon how you feel about clay you can then either turn the mass with a tool, or tread the clay with bare feet to expose new wet surfaces, both to the air and to the absorbent surface beneath. Remember, the basic aim is to change the state of

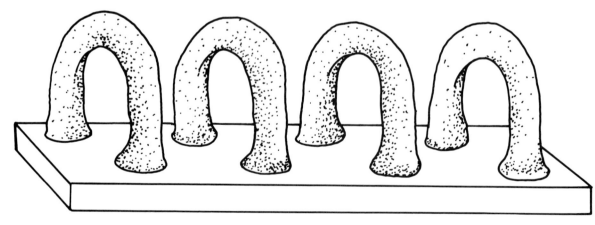

Loops of wet clay stiffening on a plank.

Rolled to show firm outer crust with soft clay pockets.

may even have been put through a pug-mill, which thoroughly mixes and de-airs the clay, and will then have been stored in thick coils of two, three or four inch (5, 7.5 or 10cm) diameter according to the size of the machine. With luck, the clay is then ready for use.

Assuming no mechanical aid, wedging and kneading are vital. Clay which has not been sufficiently prepared will inevit-ably cause frustration and heartache, even though the real cause of a problem may not be understood. Difficulties ex-perienced when attempting to throw pots on a wheel may well be due to inadequate preparation of the body rather than the potter's inability to grasp the essential skills. Lack of experience of clay itself can sometimes be the cause of difficulties elsewhere.

The dilemma facing the potter is sim-ple. Is it worthwhile spending time and effort kneading clay, when one could be practising on the wheel or getting on with some form of building? As can be seen from what I have said so far, clay will not necessarily be in an ideal condi-tion for the intended use. Whether it has just been taken from a plastic bag, ex-truded from a pugmill or simply dumped out of a soak-bin, chances are it will not be 'right'. Many students have fought lumps of ill-prepared clay in vain attempts to produce something, only to experience the double frustration of non-achievement and the sneaking thought that time spent in preparation might have given rise to a more fulfilling out-come. If there is ever a potter's rule which should be carved on a tablet of stone, it is 'Thoroughly prepare your clay'.

the clay from a sloppy mess to self-supporting plasticity. In other words, the clay should be firm enough not to spread out if unsupported, nor be so wet that it will stick like glue to everything with which it is in contact.

If the drying out or stiffening up pro-cess has been carried out successfully it should now be possible to 'wedge' con-veniently sized lumps of the clay to obtain the ultimate – a homogeneous mass or body of clay containing no air bubbles, foreign bodies, or hard or soft lumps of clay within the whole. At evening classes slopping out and initial drying will often have been carried out for you. The clay

PREPARING CLAY FOR RE-USE

Preparing clay for re-use really is not as difficult or time consuming as you might imagine. Let us assume that a lump of clay has been reclaimed to the state where it is not too sticky, but is still uneven in texture and density, probably with air bubbles and pockets of slurry which need distributing evenly through the mass. It is neither potentially too wet nor too dry. You should start by wedging the clay, partly to mix and spread it, partly to identify the exact condition of the clay.

Wedging

Wedging is used to remove air pockets, to mix the clay thoroughly, to ensure consistent density, and, by allowing the

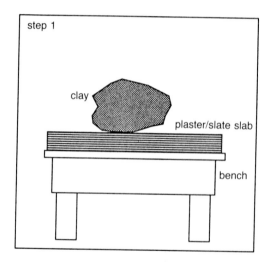

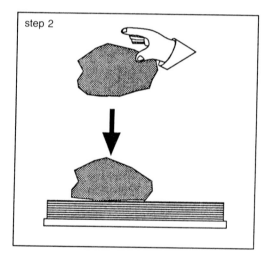

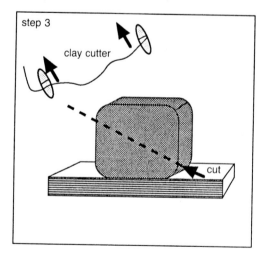

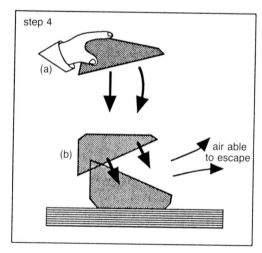

Wedging, to remove air pockets and homogenise the clay.

body to stretch, to assist the discus-shaped particles to align themselves in a common plane (as described earlier) to achieve maximum plasticity. Wedging is sometimes considered to be the first of two stages in the preparation of the clay, but it can also be used successfully on its own. It is ideal for the initial mixing of larger quantities of reclaim, of about ½cwt (25kg) or more.

Step 1

Take a lump of clay of a size you can manage, between 20 and 50lb (9–23kg) (you will only be lifting half of it most of the time) and put it on a solidly supported plaster or slate slab. If neither is available, a concrete paving slab will do.

We have found both concrete and slate inferior to plaster, however, as they are both less porous, and consequently the clay tends to stick to these surfaces more.

Step 2

Lift the lump and drop it (let gravity do the work for you where possible) from 2–3ft (60–90cm) above the bench so that it slams down and stretches outwards a little. Pick it up and turn it 90°, dropping it to form a second flat surface. Knock the lump into a block shape by dropping again to form all four sides. The lump should now be cubic, having six sides, should have a heavy dough-like movement, but should not stick either to the work surface or to your hands.

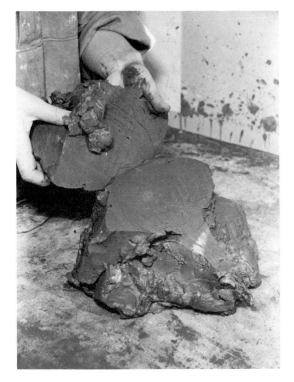

Cut and turn clay.

Lift clay.

Slam down, curved surface into cut surface, to spread and mix.

Prevent air from being trapped by avoiding 'slapping' flat surfaces together.

Step 3

Using a nylon or twisted wire clay cutter, slice through the clay, making a cut sloping up from the work surface.

Step 4

Pick up the top free part of the clay, turn it, and slam it down on to the other piece so that first, a different part of the lifted piece is now brought into contact with the lower, and second, a curved surface meets a flat surface so that no slapping noise is made when both pieces are slammed together. Noise means that air has probably been trapped between two flat surfaces; a quiet marriage of the two parts should ensure this doesn't happen.

By repeating Step 4, turning the total block through 90° regularly, it will be possible to stretch the clay and exclude air in a relatively short, if rather tiring, time. I was once told to repeat this process 200 times, or until my arms dropped off, after which the clay would be perfect. It is probably easier and more reliable to check the cross-section of clay each time you cut it. At first you will observe differences in texture on the surfaces of the clay with occasional pockets of air, some of which may be quite large. Very soon the pockets will have become much less obvious, and there will be a more uniform texture on the surfaces. When you find that no air pockets appear through the single cut, slice through again above and below the original cut and check those sections. Carefully slam the clay together again, and if all cuts are homogeneous you might consider the job complete. The clay should now be ready for use.

To make absolutely sure that the condition of your clay is perfect you should now knead the clay.

Kneading

Kneading is often problematic for a potter. The technique is similar to that of kneading dough, but do remember that your aim is exactly the opposite to the baker. Your aim is to remove air from the clay, and having wedged most out there is little point in working more back into

it. Stretch and turn the mass of clay to constantly expose fresh surfaces to the plaster work surface. This action brings air pockets to the surface and bursts them as the clay tugs and stretches against the plaster top.

There are two methods of kneading; the spiral method, and the ox-face method which produces a characteristic ox or bull head shape. Practise both ways with modest lumps of clay, so that you will later be able to use the style appropriate to the bodies and quantities you require.

Returning to the golden rule – prepare clay *thoroughly*. Another factor, often overlooked because it is so obvious, is that if the lump of clay is causing you premature exhaustion whilst kneading,

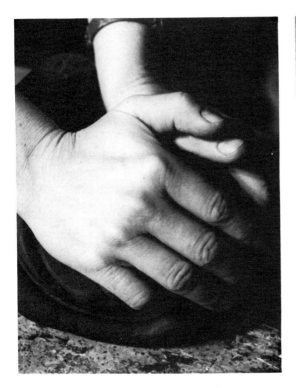

Use heels of hands to push and twist clay.

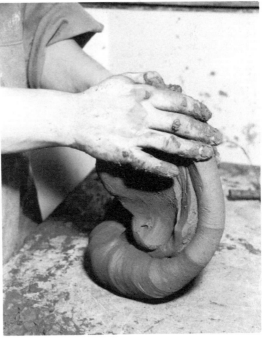

Characteristic spiral twist, which constantly exposes fresh clay, stretching and bursting air bubbles.

21

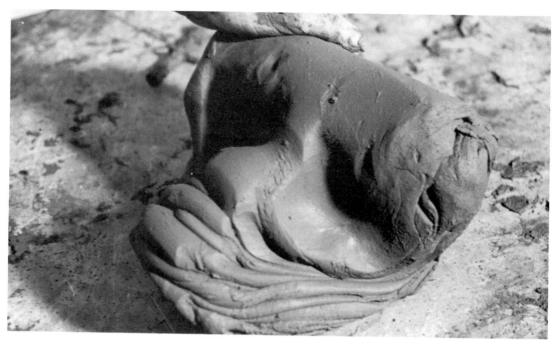

Ox- or monkey-face, two-handed spiral technique.

The material kneaded into a single spiral.

the fact is that if it cannot be kneaded, it will not be thrown. Of course the reverse is also true. If the clay kneads easily it is probably in splendid condition for throwing. In fact if the clay is rather on the stiff side it would have been difficult to wedge properly, too. If the condition of the clay can be diagnosed at that early stage, a considerable amount of effort can be saved.

Water cannot easily be added to plastic clay, so if your lump of clay seems too hard to prepare properly, the best way to soften it is to add softer clay. Slice up the harder lump, spreading or placing a layer of soft clay between, building up a pile of

alternate soft and hard layers. Consolidate the pile, turn it on its side so that the strata are now vertical, and slice again as shown in the diagram below.

If no soft clay is available there is no alternative but to resort to water. Clay does not readily absorb water, except on its surface, so if water is to be added, as large a surface area as possible should be presented. By making use of the slicing technique above and ensuring that the whole is sliced very thinly, it is possible to further increase the surface area by piercing the sliced lump with a thin stick or the long handle of an artist's paint brush so that water poured gently over

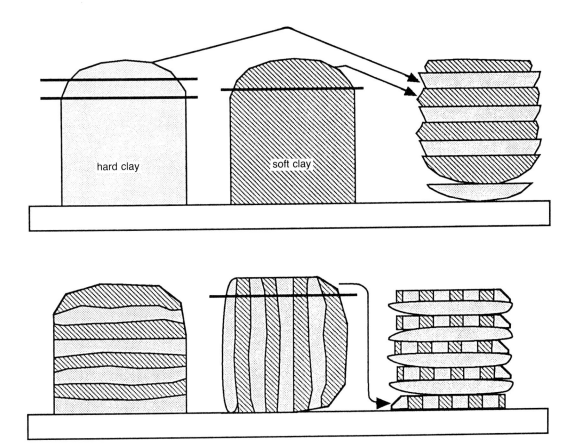

Softening hard clay by the 'slicing' technique.

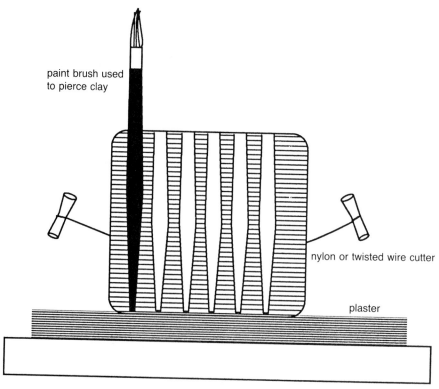

paint brush used
to pierce clay

nylon or twisted wire cutter

plaster

Piercing the sliced clay, and pouring water into the holes, will also help in clay softening.

the clay will percolate down through the vertical holes and out through horizontal cuts, wetting a considerable area.

This method produces very wet, slippery slices of clay which, when turned and cut at right angles, become a soggy mass of diced up cubes. These will be difficult to turn and press into a consolidated lump at first, but persevere. After a short period of apparent hopeless chaos the clay will begin to form up into a reasonably manageable lump again, and by initially wedging and later kneading, an improvement in overall condition will take place. It may be that the process has to be repeated before a satisfactory consistency has been achieved, but the improvement *can* be made.

Variations on these procedures can be used to blend different bodies, introduce body stains, colouring oxides, sands or grogs, bearing in mind that dry ingredients will stiffen the body, so it is worth wetting out any additive which is to be of significant quantity.

STORAGE

Exactly the same storage problems exist for reclaimed clays as for new, bought in clays, so the same procedures need to be followed. The only real difference is that the bags of new clay will not necessarily be required immediately, whereas some if not all of the hard-won reclaim may be.

After further preparing the clay for immediate use, as will be discussed later, the remainder can be stored safely in an airtight container. It is the clay required immediately that could possibly be at risk. Do make sure that you carefully cover up *all* clay not in actual use. A ball of clay left open to the air for only a short time will start to stiffen on its most exposed surfaces, and will then prove difficult to centre when put on the wheel. All that is needed is a polythene bag or sheet tucked around the clay so that it is readily at hand, but protected from the drying effects of heat or draughts. Balls of clay stored overnight, or longer, often lose moisture even when well wrapped. This again results in uneven consistency and so it is advisable only to weigh out sufficient clay for the one working session. Care is necessary at all stages of production, and when applied will amply repay you in terms of results.

IN CONCLUSION

1 Store clay in airtight containers whenever possible.
2 Always prepare clay (by wedging or kneading) prior to use.
3 Protect it from drying out in the air when in use.

Observe the above and work to a system appropriate for yourself, and you will go a long way to overcoming some of the niggling problems you would otherwise encounter. As a bonus it will encourage the development of a deeper sympathy of and for the medium, and will transform the seemingly irksome task of preparation into an integral part of the craft process. You will be reassured in the knowledge that you can control and determine the outcome of your efforts, and you will be freer to concentrate on the creative aspects of your work.

3 Elements of Design

Whereas many books, and I suspect many courses, catering for the novice potter are rightly concerned with the practical problems of actually making artefacts, frequently little or no consideration is given to the factors of design. In other instances the aesthetics of ceramics is discussed in esoteric eloquence, and this can be as confusing or unhelpful to the uninitiated as not discussing the subject at all. The simple fact is that we cannot make anything without in some way considering design. In other words it is not a case of being obliged to take design into account but rather that it is impossible to make something *without* doing so. Design is implicit in the making process. Design is included here before methods are discussed in an attempt to promote a consciousness of it throughout subsequent discussion of practical techniques.

In producing a piece of pottery we are concerned, as in all other areas of design activity, with two basic factors:

1   Form – which is concerned with how an object looks. Is it elegant? Interesting? Does it enhance or detract?
2   Function – which poses questions of utility. What is it? What is it required to do? Is it capable of doing so? Does it work?

Both factors are directly related to the method by which the object is to be made. Surface decoration can enhance form or disguise it; in some instances a glazed surface will enhance the function of a form. Although it can be convenient to compartmentalise, however, isolating either form or function for the purposes of identifying specific design problems, it is also true that the two are inexorably interconnected. The visual appearance of a teapot's spout cannot be judged without reference to the teapot's shape and the spout's effect on the overall appearance. And however appropriate the form of the spout might be, it will still be unacceptable if it will not pour. In a similar way, if a conceived design cannot be produced by the method chosen, or for some technical reason will not fire without problems, the aesthetics of the design will have to be reconsidered.

FORM

Form should be considered in conjunction with the proposed method of production; in other words, is the form to be wheel-thrown or made from flat slabs of clay. It should also take into account the changes and stresses imposed upon the material, and hence structure, of the artefact when drying and particularly during firing. Forces acting upon (if not against) your pot are:

Shrinkage Both during the initial drying out stage and when being fired.

Expansion When the temperature of a body is increased, the body expands. An obvious point but, coupled with shrinkage, unique tensions develop wherein a clay body is expected to both shrink and expand at the same time. Is it any wonder that we refer to the 'ordeal by fire'?

Whilst your ware is undergoing these traumatic changes during firing, kiln furniture such as shelving is probably (although made of ceramic material) only expanding and contracting. Any shrinkage will have already taken place during its manufacture. The result is that the movement of a ware's supporting shelves will be different to that of the pot. It is worth considering this latter point when producing objects which require firing because, particularly with heavy, flat wares, there could be additional stresses imposed upon the ware by conflicting rates of expansion and contraction. This causes 'drag', the foot of a pot contracting at a different rate to that of its supporting shelf. This will possibly damage a piece unable to move with the shelf (*see* below).

The problem can be solved by making a narrower foot to the ware, allowing

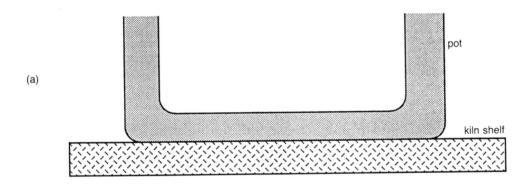

(a)

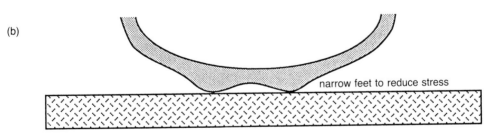

(b)

(a) The weight of the pot pressing down on to its base prevents independent movement. There is 100 per cent contact and friction with the kiln shelf. The pot will look rather earthbound. (b) A narrow foot reduces stress at the base when pot and shelf are expanding or contracting at different rates. Reduced points of contact mean that if the foot is a quarter of the overall width of the pot, the problems of shrinkage and friction are reduced to a quarter. Also, light is allowed under the pot, giving it a lighter appearance.

maximum natural unstressed expansion and contraction. Reference will also be made to this in Chapter 9 when discussing firing.

It is tempting for beginners to produce large flat forms, possibly with slabbed walls, first because it seems easy, and second because such forms can be purchased from the mass production outlets. But it is worth remembering that the objects you make must survive the kiln if your efforts are not to be wasted. In an industrial pottery an almost inert 'paste' would have been used, especially developed for a specific firing schedule. We, as craft potters, use real clays. So as in most design situations we have to compromise. Before looking at what you can actually do, let us look again at the shrinkage/form problem in a theoretical sense, and at the basic shapes available to potters.

Shapes

Although there are literally millions of subtly different shapes produced by the potter there are only three basic ones from which all others are derived – cylinder, cone and sphere. These are often combined to produce a composite form,

but let us examine them first in their simplest terms.

As potters we work in three dimensions. These three-dimensional basic shapes, however, can be reduced to two dimensions, giving three profile shapes:

3-D	2-D
cylinder	square or rectangle
cone	triangle
sphere	circle

This rather obvious idea can be applied to the design of pots in terms both of structure and aesthetics. As the diagram below illustrates, a circle has only one dimension, a square has only two and, for the purposes of simplicity, so has the rectangle. A triangle has three dimensions. The latter is the most complex shape and is open to a vast range of permutations in terms of relative dimensions, whereas the circle, and indeed the sphere, have only one – the radius.

Structurally, the sphere is the perfect shape. Stresses on its form, either shrinkage or expansion and contraction will be evenly distributed given that, if made in

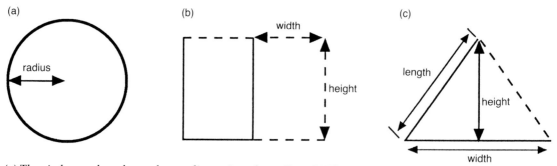

(a) The circle or sphere has only one dimension, the radius. (b) The square and rectangle have two dimensions, height and width. (c) The triangle/cone has three dimensions, height, width of base and length of side.

ceramic, the thickness of the wall is even. Its dynamic tensions are in equilibrium. In a similar way, a cylindrical tube will be less prone to stress than one with a square section made with the same amount of material. Having only one dimension, the sphere is also aesthetically beyond reproach.

Unfortunately this perfect ceramic form cannot be left in its perfect state and subjected to the fire. Air trapped inside would expand at a great rate when heated, exploding the form, even if it had not cracked when trapped air became compressed due to the initial shrinkage arising from its drying out. So it has to have a hole somewhere to allow air to expand and escape. This of course does not present a problem, because pots usually require holes of some sort in order to fulfil function. But the form will also require at least a modestly flattened foot in order to prevent it rolling about during firing and later as a finished object. Glazing would also be a problem. The form which now suggests itself is a compromise between the ideal sphere and a flat-footed cylinder or cone. The degree of compromise will be determined by aesthetic considerations and those of function:

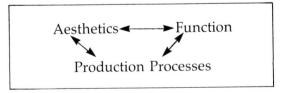

The simple model above indicates the interrelationship between three areas or factors which significantly influence outcomes of the design process.

Function

As an illustration of the process outlined above, let us attempt to design a simple dish. Most people would know what a dish is and what it does. It is nevertheless useful to note that:

1   A dish is a container, usually shallow, not necessarily circular, used for serving or containing foodstuffs.
2   It could be used for cooking, i.e. oven-to-table ware.
3   When not used as above it could be used as a decorative feature, having an open interior inviting some form of decoration.

From the above we could now start to visualise some sort of design based on a plan-view, possibly combining a basic mixture of circle and rectangle or square (*see* plan over). By dividing this plan into quarter segments and developing alternative profiles as per sections (a), (b), (c), and (d) it is possible to select what seems to provide the most interesting or pleasing outline. By using the selected quarter section, modifying it as necessary, it is now possible to come up with scores of slightly different shapes.

My own feeling is that curves should somehow flow, blending together, without awkward joins or excessively tight corners. It will probably be found that clay has similar preferences, particularly when the third dimension of the dish, the depth, is considered. All we have so far is a plan-view. In order to complete the basic design profiles, cross-sections for length and breadth are also necessary. This could be achieved by simple measurement. If the selected plan is 9 × 14in (23 × 35cm) overall, perhaps a

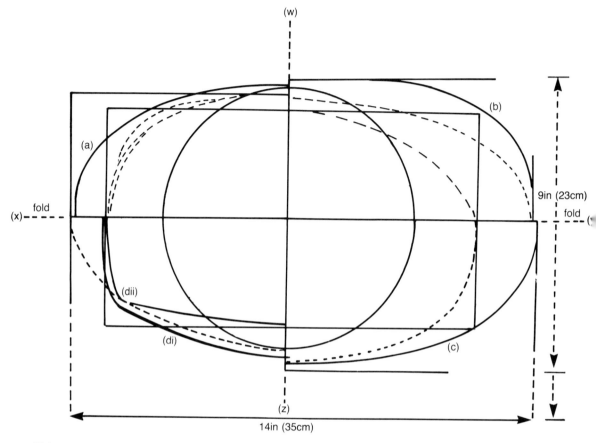

Using quarters of a plan, select a profile and trace it off using folded detail paper.

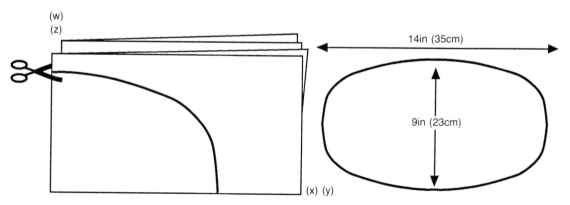

Cut the plan view out of the folded detail paper. Opening out the paper, determine the length and breadth of your pot.

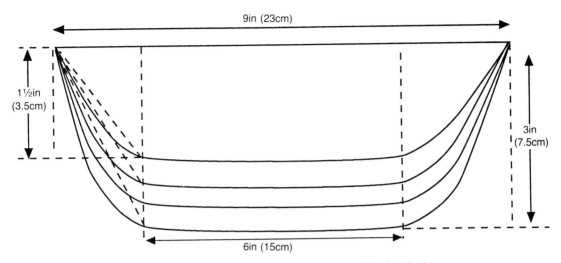

9in (23cm)

1½in (3.5cm)

3in (7.5cm)

6in (15cm)

Choice of cross-section is also important to the overall appearance of the finished pot.

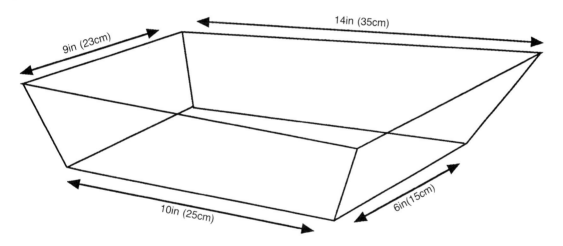

14in (35cm)

9in (23cm)

6in(15cm)

10in (25cm)

The above plan indicates in general terms the proportions of the dish.

bottom or foot measurement could be about 6 × 10in (15 × 25cm).

Obviously the depth has also to be considered. Possibly something like 3in (7.5cm) would do. Or a similar plan to that on page 32 could be constructed (*see* plan below).

In keeping with the idea of flowing outlines, so the cross-sections should flow also. A gentle curve will probably serve best; perhaps the shallower version with a narrow, modified foot would be suitable. The question now arises, though, how exactly will such a dish be made? Two methods of producing this sort of dish will be described and illustrated in Chapter 6. You will see that there are clear links between function, form and the method of producing the article.

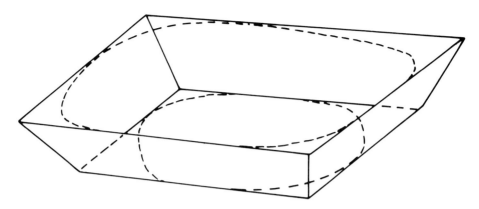

This is the previous plan, with depth reduced and plan view profiles superimposed.

When examining design factors in this way it may seem that problems exist which, from a pessimistic point of view, appear to dampen if not dispel one's initial enthusiasm for making something. But builders recognise the need for adequate foundations, athletes prepare carefully for their events and climbers and mountaineers plan and prepare for their expeditions very carefully in advance; all this preparation to avoid defeat, or at least disappointment, later. No potter, novice or expert, expects to design out all the problems that might be encountered during the often exacting process between conception of an object and its ultimate emergence from the fire. What you can do, though, is overcome obvious pitfalls.

Returning to the basic shapes for a little longer, I mentioned the ideal form of the sphere. But what about others?

The Cylinder

The basic shape produced on a potter's wheel is the cylinder. Students are usually encouraged to master this basic form before moving on to more complex shapes. Let us then compare it to a sphere, and also a simple cone (*see* figure opposite). It has been suggested that ceramic design is probably the purest form of abstract art. Certainly we are concerned with pure, simple relationships between dimensions such as height, breadth and width. In figure (a) opposite there are only two dimensions to be married together into a cylinder of pleasing proportion; figure (d) shows the multiplicity of dimensions where three simple cones have been combined. Where radii are raised or lowered, x being the radius in question, the possibilities for profile change are increased, as are the problems of proportion. If a general 'feel' for the overall design can be conceived as a basis for development as work progresses it will not matter that the finished piece is not exactly identical to an overworked original drawing. It is quite usual, in any case, for potters to design by selection. Make a series and choose the form that seems somehow special when compared to the others in the range. If your choice does not coincide with that of someone else it hardly matters; aesthetic considerations are

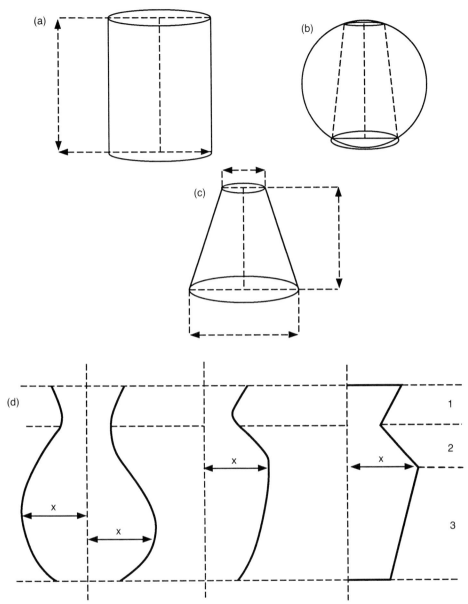

A simple cylinder (a) has two measurements – height and radius. In profile it appears as a square or rectangle. In the case of rectangles, proportion of height to width is a straightforward relationship which can be subtle or crude. For an in-depth examination of this sort of relationship you may wish to refer to the 'golden mean' rule. In a simple cone (b), relationships are increased, i.e. width of top to width of bottom, width of top to height, width of bottom to height. If height is altered so are the angles of the sides. Even when modified (c), a sphere has a more complex set of relationships or proportions as in (b) above. Such relationships determine the character or nature of the form. As a form becomes more complex (d), so the relationships between dimensions increase. The three cones combined to form a vase provide almost unlimited permutations. Variations on this theme appear as amphorae, English medieval jugs and universally produced vase forms from antiquity to the present day.

based as much upon personal preferences and insights as upon informed opinion as to what is or is not acceptable.

Stresses within a form will relate to proportion in a rather different way. A very shallow cylinder with low, wide sides on a broad base will probably be more affected by the effects of shrinkage, expansion and contraction than will a narrower, taller and hence more supported shape (*see* below). Generally, wheel-thrown vessels will probably be less susceptible to stress than will slab-built pieces, which will be looked at in depth in Chapter 6

Fortunately there is another aspect of thrown pottery worth bearing in mind. It is neither desirable nor likely that pots thrown on a wheel will be, in engineering terms, exact cylinders. Nor will they be exactly even in thickness. If you examine the work of experienced craftspersons you will almost certainly discover various 'faults' which are actually built-in

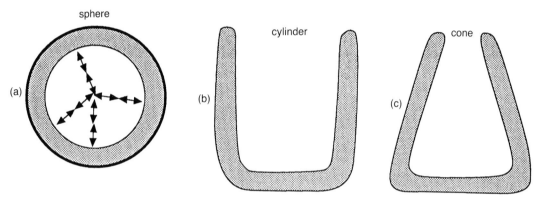

Stresses within a form. (a) Sphere has stresses distributed equally throughout the form. (b) Cylinder has strong support at foot but open end is much less supported. (c) Cone is less likely to distort at lip. Could pull in slightly at its 'waist'.

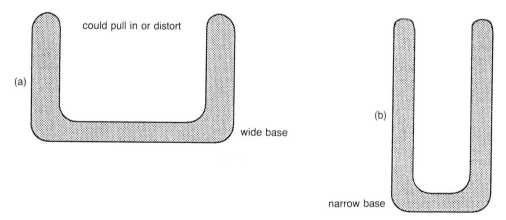

Stresses on a cylinder. (a) Short and wide. The foot could stress, when in contact with the kiln shelf. (b) Tall and narrow. This is a stronger form. The narrow base is less susceptible to damage from stress, and there is no excessive stress at the lip.

features intended to offset problems such as those already mentioned. A straight cylinder may be given a very slight convex profile to insure against a concave curve developing. It might also be given a slight thickening of the lip, possibly with a hint of a neck. Such features add both vitality and stability to the form. They will also be as much the result of a human hand working with the living clay, as with a desire to design out construction problems.

In much the same way a broad-bottomed gratin dish will have soft, subtle lines as it were to absorb possible distortion. An applied coil, possibly flattened and/or impressed, could be added to decorate and support the rim. This sort of applied support and decoration can be seen in numerous examples of contemporary and historical ceramic artefacts. Perhaps it is worth suggesting here that often it is the addition of apparently frivolous or at least unnecessary knobs, handles, bushes, animals

and the like that raises the piece from the ordinary to the extraordinary and transforms the mundane into the unique. If the object is visually more stimulating it is likely to give greater pleasure to the user, as well as possibly enhancing structural stability.

By working sympathetically with the medium you will develop a sense of what looks right or wrong. You will instinctively know that the form 'feels' right; that it works. This instinct for what is right can be developed, among other means, by using a sketchbook to explore the possibilities of form, shape and appropriate decorative designs. You will also develop an awareness of form relative to the method you select for producing an object. But whatever you make it is well to remember that you are not in competition with machines. Your chosen medium is living plastic clay and your tools are essentially hands and fingers, aided as necessary with simple extensions of those hands.

4 Setting up your Workshop or Studio

Any potter who has moved house, and therefore workshop, will tell you that moving house is easy. It is the other part which hurts. Most people with their own workshops would find it difficult to list all the items contained in them, all of which they consider essential to the production of their work. This is due in part at least to our collecting things as we go along, appropriate to special needs we identify according to the sort of work we produce and the particular means by which it is produced. As will be seen, however, there is no need for an elaborate array of expensive tools or equipment if you wish to work at home, whether in the kitchen or in a purpose-built or converted room, shed or outbuilding. Some items are essential, some will become desirable or necessary to extend the range of possibilities within the activity, other things may become embarrassingly expensive white elephants once purchased, and take up valuable space in the workshop.

Whether the proposed workshop is to be used by only one person working at home or is the foundation for a specialist provision in a school there will be a need for clay storage and preparation and for a place in which to fire it. A potter's wheel would also be a likely requirement. A suitable work surface is necessary and a storage system must be developed.

CLAY

If we look at the basic requirements first it will be seen that clay, as it arrives in polythene bags, presents no real problem. Plastic or galvanised metal dustbins are useful; alternatively the original bags could be stacked or double-wrapped until required. Once opened, rather more care should be exercised to prevent clay drying out, so it needs to be protected from air and heat. Store it in a cool, ideally damp, place away from the kiln and keep it airtight. Kept in this way clay will actually improve its plasticity.

Once the clay has been used, a system will have to be devised. A surprising amount of clay does not actually make it to the kiln. Some of this will be wet, some of it dried out, and some will have been handled so that it is no longer plastic enough to be reused unless recycled. First, then, a plastic bowl, or just a plastic bag, will serve to gather up the reclaim. With care, the soft could be put in with stiffer, but not dry, clay so that it consolidates a little, ready to be kneaded up again. The harder clay is best allowed to dry out completely before recyling, as described on pages 14 to 25. A second container therefore becomes necessary.

Where reclaim is kept to a minimum by diligently attending to scraps as they occur, it should be relatively easy to avoid excessive heaps of reclaim later.

Reclaim brings with it its own storage problems in any event. Using a reasonably tight system based on the above it would be possible to keep on top of any recycling, even in a school where no technician or pugmill are available to reduce the load.

SHELVING

All the marvellous pots produced will need shelving on which they can dry out slowly and safely, and be stored before and after firing. A damp cupboard is also an asset for the storage of items which must be kept moist prior to completion later. Again the plastic bag could be used to good effect where such a special item is not available. Any cupboard space would be useful, either as an aid to maintaining pots in the leatherhard state, or to protect pots' surfaces from dust.

KILNS

When pieces have been completely dried out there has to be some means of firing them. Different types of kiln and the techniques of firing them will be discussed in some depth in other chapters. So I will talk in general terms for the moment, and would suggest that visits to local colleges or schools with good ceramics facilities might well be worthwhile, as would contact with local potters. The latter in particular are often justifiably proud of their kilns, which are often self-built, and will usually be prepared to discuss merits, and indicate drawbacks as experienced first hand.

First do some careful research. Then obtain a kiln suited to your requirements.

If you only wish to produce ceramic jewellery your needs will easily be met by a small test-kiln using electricity and requiring only a domestic thirteen amp socket. If you intend to produce pots or sculptural pieces and hope to sell enough at least to break even on the cost of your hobby it would be sensible to go for a larger kiln at the outset.

Your choice of kiln depends to a great extent on what you want to do with your kiln, what you can, or will be able, to afford, and where you are planning to site it. Electric kilns are nowadays quick and clean-firing, are relatively easy to install, with professional help, and can be fitted with easy-to-use mechanical or microprocessor control units at very reasonable cost.

Gas-fired kilns are an obvious alternative. Basically there are two types; models that consume normal domestic gas from the mains supply, and others designed to burn bottled liquid gas. The latter burns more cleanly and does not create dangerous gaseous by-products requiring tall chimneys to exhaust them safely. On the other hand, piped-in gas is convenient once installed, and is likely to be less costly in the long term. Technical advice is always available from your local gas board and should be sought well in advance of installation. Apart from the possible cost of getting a supply to the kiln site it is wise to check with them what extra equipment may be required, and also the likely cost. If the conventional alternatives do not appeal, you may be tempted to consider building a wood-fired kiln. In some areas fuel may be both cheap and plentiful, but both construction and firing are labour-intensive. A first successful firing will probably be more than adequate reward for the expended effort, but if reliable, consistent and economical firings are needed this last way is unlikely to be as satisfactory as the others.

WHEELS

Some sort of wheel is the other most basic requirement. Whether or not you actually need one again depends on what you intend to produce. Cost is also a very real consideration because, like kilns, there are wheels for all occasions. When purchasing a wheel it is worth remembering that it will have to be capable of working with you for however long you continue to produce wheel-thrown pots. Size of wheel does not determine size of pot, but price will often reflect the quality and design specifications of a machine which will either work well throughout its lifetime, or will be a source of discomfort, frustration and irritation if it is simply not capable of doing the job required of it. Enrolment to an evening class should provide an opportunity to use different wheels; try them for personal 'fit', and to discover how well the different types function under load.

OTHER ESSENTIALS

In addition to the three major items mentioned above there are other items essential either to the production of wares or for the well-being and convenience of the potter. A strong work-bench is required for the production of hand-built pieces, and for clay preparation. If space allows, a bench for each is an advantage. The plaster slab and any slop will then not

hinder making and finishing, and there will be less likelihood of dry scraps of clay being accidentally mixed in with soak. A sink and running water are also very useful, although it is possible to manage without if they are available reasonably close to the workshop.

It would be inappropriate here to list all the other items it is possible to gather together. With clay, kiln and work surface a start can be made. As work progresses, minor items will be thought more necessary and can be acquired at that time. There can be no definitive list in any case, due to the nature of work and individual preferences. Instead I shall indicate the tools and equipment required to carry out tasks and projects covered in other sections as they come up.

LAYOUT

Layout of the work area is worth some thought. If you are starting completely

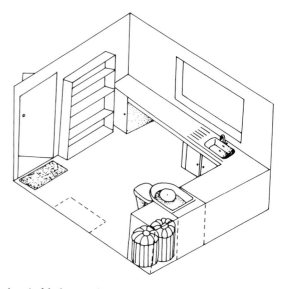

A suitable layout for a workshop.

from scratch such things as power points, lighting, sink and even windows can be placed for maximum convenience. Where some existing facilities are to be utilised without alteration, to a lesser or greater extent the way equipment is eventually arranged will be determined by these factors. Light is probably the most important of these. Try to arrange things so that natural daylight is available, particularly for detailed work. A good source of light helps to highlight texture, pattern and form, as well as lessening potential eye strain.

Opposite is an illustration of a workshop area. The kilns and most materials are stored in the adjacent area, which can be better ventilated and does not require insulation. We have installed insulation in our studio section to avoid frost-damage to pots in the winter. This has also made our studio a more attractive proposition to us on a cold winter's evening. Most sheds, garages or other out-houses tend to be less than ideal in terms of comfort, and a little time and energy spent on draught-proofing and insulation is worthwhile in our experience.

5 Equipment and Tools

EQUIPMENT

Wheels

The wheel is not absolutely necessary to the ceramic process. That it seems synonymous with pots and potters, however, cannot be denied. It could be said to be the personification of the craft, and it certainly holds a fascination for anyone who becomes involved in pottery. If, like thousands of potters before, you have been moved to accept the challenge of the wheel, then the type of wheel you first encounter could be either a positive aid or a hindrance to your aspirations. A well-designed and solidly made wheel is essential in this respect and first attempts are usually more successful when working on an electrically powered wheel. There are, however, some less sophisticated types which are well worth looking at individually as they all have special qualities which can give them the edge over less effective power wheels.

Basically, a wheel can be just what its name implies. A circular slab of stone or other heavy material, pivoted on its axis so that it can revolve freely in a horizontal plane, sometimes let into the floor, has often been used. This enables the potter to sit before it, working in a convenient position, seated on the floor, and using a stick inserted into notches in the wheel's surface to set it in motion. The wheel's weight is usually heavy enough to provide sufficient momentum to allow a small pot to be thrown without the need for further applications of the stick.

Kickwheels

A rather more sophisticated version of this primitive but effective piece of equipment is widely used today. The momentum kickwheel, sometimes referred to as the 'continental wheel', has a horizontal fly wheel which turns a smaller wheelhead above it sharing the same axis, and therefore the same axle. This connecting shaft revolves in bearings supported by a rigid frame which can also carry a seat and splash-tray as illustrated below.

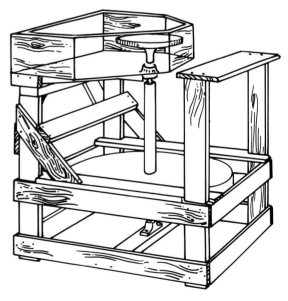

A momentum kickwheel.

On this particular model the thrower sits comfortably behind the wheel, propelling the flywheel around by driving it with thrusts of the right foot. The other foot can be placed firmly on the left horizontal support to brace the body, allowing extra thrust. The obvious disadvantage of this type of wheel is that it is incapable of handling very heavy loads. I consider this to be outweighed, however, by a number of significant advantages. It is certainly less expensive than a powered wheel if purchased ready-made, and any self-sufficient potter can construct a wheel on similar lines, making use of reclaimed material, reducing cost still further. An old lorry wheel, weighted by the addition of concrete cast into it, and placed on a stout frame capable of withstanding the considerable stresses likely to be imposed upon it makes an extremely effective wheel costing little more than the price of the bearings, fittings and perhaps a purpose-made wheelhead. Such a wheel requires no electrical facility and uses no power except that of your leg. There will be virtually no maintenance and it will be wonderfully quiet when in use. The working pace is peaceful too, with no sense of urgency. These wheels may lack the power to tackle heavy loads of clay but for jobs of modest size, soup bowls, mugs and vase forms, they are more than adequate.

From this basic momentum wheel a number of versions have been developed which include some sort of gearing and treadle system in order to improve speed, power and continuing momentum. The better versions are very good, but some models at the lower end of the price range are in fact considerably less convenient than the basic model. As a general rule a flywheel should be in the region of 100lb (45kg) in weight, and if 'freewheeling' is preferred, systems which have too many moving parts should be avoided. The frenetic rattling and clanking of these will not only absorb effort uselessly but will also irritate enormously. Treat sales claims with caution, therefore; test potential purchases under load and try to compare the various products currently available before committing yourself.

Any awkwardness you experience when first using a momentum kickwheel will soon be overcome, particularly if you adopt the freewheel tactic – never throw while kicking. Thrusting movement with a leg will be transmitted up into the thorax and arms causing difficulty at the point of contact with your clay. Set the wheel in motion at the required speed for the job, then put both feet firmly up out of the way before setting to work on the clay. The natural reduction in momentum will often match up with the speed required as the pot grows and develops, and any changes in speed, up or down, will inevitably be gentle, avoiding trauma to both clay and potter. It is this simple facility which makes the kickwheel so attractive.

Power Wheels

If the preference is for a powered wheel, then again there is a wide range of choice available. Obviously price is often the first consideration but as in the case of geared kick wheels, some models will have fewer vices than others. The basic requirements remain the same; a comfortable working position, more than adequate power, or torque, smooth operation and sensitive control. Other features, such as the ability to turn the wheelhead freely when out of gear, or not under power, may also be desirable. My big electric wheel, for example, cannot freewheel although it is marvellous in most other respects. If you intend to set up a modest workshop at home a useful compromise might be to do your throwing at a local college where they provide really first-rate equipment, and to opt for a momentum kickwheel of your own later.

Second-hand electric wheels can often be purchased relatively cheaply. A minor but significant problem here is that the model might be obsolete. Parts may not be available in some instances and in others the manufacturer may no longer

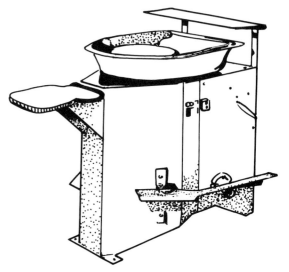

An electric cone wheel.

be in business. If you have some skill in simple engineering, and can mend and make do, most repairs will be possible. Some particularly unique mechanical features, on the other hand, may not. The safest procedure is probably to look into the manufacturer, and possibly seek the advice of someone who has had experience of wheels in the past. There are likely to be some very good bargains in old electrical wheels, and remember – electric motors are much easier to repair or replace than the odd patent gadget originally fitted to overcome some shortcoming within the design specification. Most things are, after all, a compromise between the desirable and the affordable, and wheels are no exception.

The criteria by which wheels may be judged are much the same for power-driven models as they are for kickwheels. It usually follows that the more expensive, professional models are likely to be more comfortable and convenient to work at, and will give long and trouble-free service. Without attempting to

A geared kickwheel.

turn this into a consumer report, some guidance may help you in your choice. Electric power wheels are often fitted with some sort of friction drive. Two opposed conical metal flywheels were fitted to the heavier industrial wheel, allowing for plenty of power, torque, smooth operation, and a freewheeling facility. More recently, friction drive has made use of lighter and more readily worn systems also. Some wheels rely on direct drive, speed being adjusted via the motor. This can cause erratic speed control, lack of freewheeling, and a reliance on electrical rather than purely mechanical devices. There are very handy electric wheels to be found at the more modest end of the price range but, as is often the case, purchasing the very cheapest can prove less economical in the long run.

When purchasing a wheel of any sort it is worth checking on how (if at all) the wheelhead is removed. Probably the best system is where the head is left-hand screw threaded to fit on to the drive shaft. It thereby lightens itself up when under load and requires a sharp tug to loosen and unscrew it. Some means of preventing the flywheel from turning helps; sometimes a firmly placed foot will suffice. Another system uses a simple locking system, as illustrated below.

Wear can cause an irritating minor problem symptomised by a slight knocking movement at the wheelhead when under load, especially when clay is being centred. This is compensated for by the ease of removing the head. Tapered male/female fitting is sometimes encountered. These can be rather difficult to remove, however.

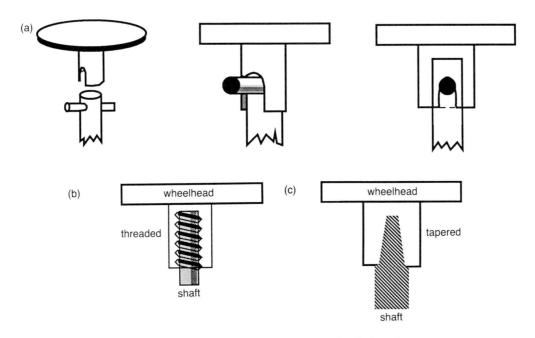

Removable wheelheads. (a) Key system. This locks down on to the shaft and locates on to a dowel key via the notch in the wheelhead shaft. (b) Screw system. The action of throwing tightens the thread. (c) Tapered male/female fittings.

The main advantage of having a removable wheelhead is that heads of varying diameter can be used. Normally you do not remove it just to take off a large bowl or plate, but it is always an asset to be able to if necessary. Another consideration particularly significant in schools and colleges is that a removable head facilitates cleaning.

Kilns

Fire is fundamental to the ceramic process, and from earliest times up to the present day pottery makers have used it. With the advent of electricity, however, firing pots has become cleaner, more convenient, and much more easily undertaken by the occasional potter. It is more widely used nowadays than traditional natural and fossil fuels such as wood or oil. With the development of highly sophisticated control units making use of microprocessors it is now possible to remove not only flame, smoke and soot but also toil, sweat and tears from the firing process. Which, it might be argued, also removes the craftsman potter away from intimate contact with the total ceramic experience.

Before discussing what are after all the most recent developments in the evolution of ceramic technology it is perhaps worth remembering that electric kilns are in a category of their own. Although they, like any other kiln, consume energy and produce heat, there is no fire as such. The ultimate design of such kilns is therefore significantly different from other types, as is their functioning. Their major advantages are their cleanliness, convenience of firing and ease of installation.

Kilns which do make use of fire, and could be considered traditional rather than hi-tech, range from the basic and simple to the very sophisticated. Before discussing particular types of natural fuel-fired kilns, however, the basic principles of kiln design should be considered.

Clay has to be subjected to considerable heat in order to change it irreversibly into the new ceramic material. The heat generated at the centre of a bonfire is certainly capable of effecting this metamorphosis, but pots fired in such a way are exposed to a number of dangers and risks if simply placed upon the ground with fire built around. For instance, the foot of a pot will receive very little heat. If several pots are fired together those on the outside of the stack will receive less heat on their outsides than those near the centre. The wares will be subjected to uneven firing and rapid changes in temperature, and will be at risk during stoking. Use of fuel would be wasteful. If an attempted glaze firing produced even half-decent results on just a few of the

Simple open fire with pots.

wares it would be the consequence of extreme good fortune rather than masterful control of the fire. I am not saying that such an exercise is not worthwhile, however, as it is always great fun, thought-provoking and instructional at the same time.

As can be seen from the diagram opposite there are at least three considerations to be taken into account when attempting to improve upon a simple bonfire. Pots need to be up above the fire where heat is greater. They may need to be protected from excessive flashing caused by direct contact with flame, from the action and results of stoking, and from falling over. It will also be necessary to distribute heat evenly throughout as far as possible.

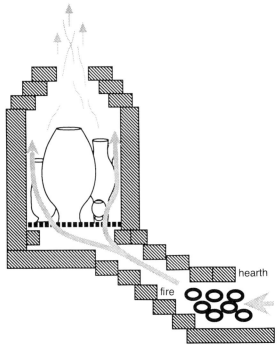

Fire enclosed by simple updraft construction.

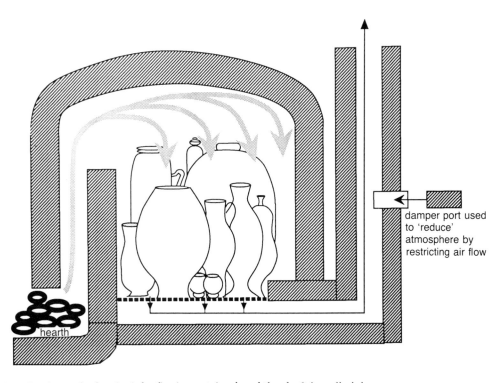

Showing the down draft principle; fire is contained and the draft is pulled down through the chamber before exiting up the chimney.

The designs of a great majority of kilns in use at the present time are really only modifications to the updraught and bottle kilns which have been in use all over the world for many centuries. Development of the downdraught kiln has taken place much more recently to improve on the efficiency of the kiln generally, and to make it easier to achieve the higher temperatures required for stoneware and porcelain. Heat is usually more evenly distributed throughout a downdraught kiln also.

Wood as a Fuel

Over the centuries wood has been the universal fuel for these traditionally designed kilns. Its advantage in the past has been that it was readily available and cheap. Nowadays, sources of fuel can be found for the potter who is prepared to organise transport and handle, dry and store the large quantities of timber necessary. But firing up a wood-fired kiln can be a long business and is labour-intensive to say the least. Fuel must be dry enough not to dampen the fire as it is added. Stoking must be carried out to achieve a steady build-up of temperature and must be continual. Perhaps more important is the size of the kiln. Wood-fired kilns are usually quite large so that the work of several months can be fired using the kiln regularly but only a few times a year.

The time required to fire up a kiln will not be directly proportional to its size. It is relatively less time consuming to fire one large kiln than it is to fire a small kiln

John Leach stoking his two-chamber climbing kiln at Muchelney Pottery.

a number of times to obtain the same volume of output. And although it will probably be more cost-effective in terms of fuel, there is in either case a storage problem which most studio potters are in no position to overcome. Most established potters envy and admire the few who do work with wood-fired kilns not only because of the evocative traditional image but also because of the special characteristics of wood-fired glaze and bodies. Whether or not you have the space to build such a kiln there are other factors to be considered before deciding on wood as a fuel. Neighbours may well object to smoke emission and planners will certainly have to be consulted before chimneys can be erected.

So what about alternatives? Coal could be used, but it is obviously dirty and much more unpleasant to handle than wood. Coal has been generally replaced by gas or electricity, which are now our main sources of energy for kiln firing. However, for some people wood's attraction remains, not just because it is traditional, or that its results are often so attractive. I, for instance, feel safe with wood; its power is controllable; it is not under pressure and neither is it invisible and potentially wayward. However, in our modern society both electricity and gas are readily and safely available.

Gas-Fired Kilns

In theory at least, our archetypal wood-fired kiln can easily be converted to gas.

Studio gas kiln.

Certainly a modified traditional design can be adapted to the new fuel – in principle there is little difference in the kiln itself. It is the means of delivering the fuel which both makes the system more sophisticated, and more conveniently operated. Fuel is either obtained from a mains supply or from bottled liquid petroleum gas (LPG) gas cylinders, and will be constantly delivered to the burners until the supply is cut off. Without going into detail here, gas is piped to burners where it is mixed with oxygen and ignited. Flame is then directed into the firing chamber using baffles, bagwalls or muffles to assist even heating and to prevent flashing on pots nearest the flame.

With the recent introduction of ceramic fibre and extremely light, low thermal mass brick it has become possible to produce light but strong kilns capable of fast and high firings. These are easy to handle and economical in use. By using these latest techniques of kiln construction it is quite easy for the handyman potter to build an extremely useful kiln for a modest outlay in cash and time.

Although mains gas could be used if a simple design was appropriately modified, it is commonplace now to make use of bottled gas which requires no compli-

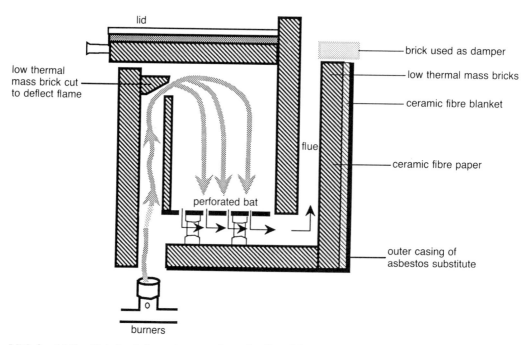

An LPG fired kiln. This basic box-structured top loading kiln requires a supportive structure to lift it sufficiently to fit burners below. Welded angle irons are ideal.

Note: The kiln drawings illustrated are intended to show general principles at work, and not as plans for construction.

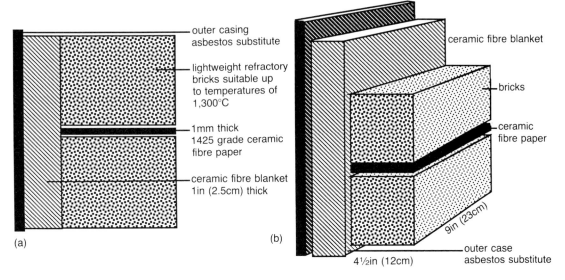

(a)

(b)

outer casing
asbestos substitute

lightweight refractory
bricks suitable up
to temperatures of
1,300°C

1mm thick
1425 grade ceramic
fibre paper

ceramic fibre blanket
1in (2.5cm) thick

ceramic fibre blanket

bricks

ceramic
fibre paper

9in (23cm)

outer case
asbestos substitute

4½in (12cm)

Sections of a low thermal mass kiln. (a) Cross-section. (b) Perspective view.

cated installation. We use a self-con-structed kiln of about four cubic feet (30cm³) of setting capacity. This is used for stoneware firings and has proved fair-ly reliable over the three years it has been in commission.

It has two burners which are fitted with flame-fail devices. These cut off the supply of gas to the burners in the event of flame failure (the flame being exting-uished by accident, usually a sudden draught), thus preventing a build-up of unignited gas within the kiln. We fire it using cones (*see* page 52) in conjunction with a pyrometer, and can increase the height of the chamber by adding an extra layer of bricks to the walls. The integral chimney impinges slightly on the setting space, but with minor alterations to the internal construction this could well be modified if necessary.

A major attraction of this type of con-struction is its simplicity. By simply building 'dry', using *no* jointing, it is possible literally to play with bricks to

discover the most suitable arrangement for walls, floor, inlet ports and spyholes so as to reduce cutting to a minimum. Where this is necessary, to shape or re-duce the size, these bricks can be cut easily using an old saw, or carved using a rasp, a coarse rasp or file, or even a knife. On the other hand, they are extremely fragile, and so must be handled with great care. They are also rather costly. This latter point is outweighed in the long term by their superb insulation properties, which reduce fuel costs con-siderably.

If you want to experience the joy and satisfaction, not to mention the excite-ment, of firing a kiln you have con-structed yourself then the new materials already mentioned should put you well on the way. Bearing in mind the com-ments made on wood firing above there is no reason why a small kiln could not be constructed for use with this fuel. On the other hand, a small gas bottle and blow-torch burner could provide a viable alternative, provided that the chamber does not greatly exceed one cubic foot $(28.3 l^3)$.

Electric Kilns

Electric kilns are extensively used and are readily available in specifications to suit the craft potter, school or industrial producer. The smallest sizes require only a thirteen amp supply and can be used on a work-bench or kitchen surface. Larger models will require the sort of supply used to power a domestic cooker. With professional assistance they can be operated from a normal supply, but larger kilns may require a separate service. All such details are provided in suppliers' catalogues.

Electric kilns are basically boxes, well insulated by a lining of high thermal insulation (HTI) or low thermal density bricks enclosing the setting chamber. Channels are carved into the brick facing to carry elements in the form of elongated wire coils or springs which produce heat when current is passed through them. Elements are arranged to deliver even distribution of heat throughout; there is no need for a chimney or other openings to introduce oxygen, and these kilns are remarkably efficient as a consequence.

Most contemporary kilns are built using extremely light refractory bricks with very low thermal conductivity. Ceramic fibre blanket is used for extra insulation and the result is an efficient kiln with fast

Front-loading electric kiln. Note three energy control knobs regulating power to upper, middle and lower elements.

Fast-fire top-loading kilns.

firing capabilities. Little heat is either lost or wasted in heating the structure of the kiln, so the cost of firings is significantly reduced compared with those incorporating traditional kiln technology.

Some points to remember if considering the purchase of a second-hand kiln are:

(a) Older kilns are more expensive to fuel than their hi-tech counterparts.

(b) Traditional construction incurs considerable weight. Even a comparatively small kiln of perhaps 2 cubic feet (56.6 l^3) capacity will require the combined strength of four or five strong persons to move it.

(c) Careful checking by a qualified electrician is advisable prior to purchase.

(d) Cost of removal, installation and replacement of damaged or missing parts and accessories could amount to almost the cost of a new model.

Having said that, second-hand kilns can be excellent value and if you are in contact with local self-sufficient potters you may well discover ways and means of maintaining an obsolete model at modest cost. For example, where replacement elements are no longer available local firms can sometimes make them to order, given the correct specifications.

All electric kilns requiring in excess of the domestic thirteen amp supply should be installed by a qualified electrician. It is also certainly desirable if not absolutely necessary to ensure that the kiln is equipped with basic safety features. An interlock system which automatically cuts off power from the elements as soon as the door is opened slightly would serve in some situations; in others it will be necessary to fit a system which both isolates the kiln when not in use and prevents the door being unlocked when power is switched on.

Any sort of electrical element will deliver its output of heat as long as it is live, charged with electricity. This being so, the temperature within the piece of equipment will increase until such time as the current is switched off or the circuit is broken due to element failure. An electric kiln, therefore, needs some sort of control facility to govern both the rate of increase in temperature and the appropriate maximum needed to fire the contents. This could of course be simply the mains switch operated manually as deemed necessary.

The obvious inconvenience of this last suggestion has led to the development of Sunvic-type energy regulator switches which can be set to turn power on for short periods of time (alternating with periods when it is turned off). Settings are marked 0 to 100, representing percentages of one minute. A setting of 50 on the dial will deliver power to the element for approximately thirty seconds in each minute. With experience of a particular kiln and switch-gear you will soon learn the settings for appropriate rates of temperature increase.

A simple alternative, used on some small kilns, quite recently, is a low–medium–high switch. This delivers power to only one, to a few, or to all elements as required so that, although switched on all the time, the increase in temperature will be gradual when only one 1 kilowatt element is live. By turning the switch to 'medium' or 'high', two and then three elements are energised, so speeding up the rate of increase by stages.

Larger studio kilns, as used in schools

Ammeter and power input control with low, medium and high settings.

and colleges, sometimes have Sunvic switches to control different banks of elements within the kiln. With experience both the rate of increase in temperature and the distribution of heat can be controlled. It would be possible for one part of a well-packed kiln to be achieving moderately high temperatures, while another would remain relatively cold, if only one circuit or element was used. By activating other elements, a more even spread of heat will be achieved, causing a quicker and more even build-up of temperature.

Temperature Control

However sophisticated the energy control, unless the temperature inside the kiln can be ascertained the operator will still have difficulty in firing it successfully. Although most people tend to think in terms of degrees centigrade what really concerns us is the amount of work done by the heat. To check this it has been the practice in the past to place rings in the kiln. They could then be withdrawn to check whether changes in the state of the body or glaze had yet taken place. If, for example, a ring showed perfectly fused glazing, then the fuel could be shut off. If the glaze remained dry or matt then the kiln was not hot enough, and the kiln would remain 'on'.

In a similar way, ceramic cones are used to check temperature (or work). These are made of refractory mixtures with varying degrees of resistance to heat, and cast into tall, slender pyramidal shapes of uniform size. When exposed to sufficient heat for the correct time these cones bend and eventually melt. By arranging cones with known characteristics within the kiln so that they can be seen through spyholes it is possible to judge the temperature at which the cones, if any, have collapsed.

A commonly used, if slightly less accurate, way of measuring temperature is to fit the kiln with a pyrometer and thermocouple. This apparatus consists of a porcelain-sheathed probe (the thermocouple), fitted through the kiln wall so that it protrudes into the firing chamber and connects via compensating cable to the pyrometer. This can be of either the traditional analogue type with needle and dial readout, or digital, with precise one degree sensitivity. Pyrometers are not as precise as cones, at least in theory. They record the actual temperature but do not indicate the amount of work done by the heat. A cone, on the other hand, responds to both heat and time. In short it will not bend if briefly exposed to its designated temperature – time is also necessary to cause the effect. In order to check heatwork it is useful to use cones in conjunction with a pyrometer.

If this seems rather too complicated, and funds are readily available, there are control units on the market which can make the process easier and more convenient in many respects. These units make use of microchip technology and provide programme facilities for any conceivable kiln-firing scenario. Once programmed, the unit will carry out a required firing schedule, switching itself on at a predetermined time and closing down when the required temperature has been reached. My own view is that where firings have to be carried out in less than ideal circumstances such units are worth their weight in gold. They can be programmed to start the schedule at a time when it would normally be impossible to do so, such as before a public building is opened, and can be relied upon to switch themselves off, again possibly when there is no potter at hand to do so. The advantage in a school situation is obvious; but other advantages are gained from using such a system. It is virtually impossible to over-fire the kiln and so expensive replacement of elements is minimised, as is stress to the brickwork. The cost of making good a couple of over-firings could easily add up to more than the cost of purchase of a 'safefire' unit. That argument alone can be convincing enough to outweigh that of higher cost. Enhanced safety of the equipment is also a positive factor.

Where funding is simply not available, but safeguards against, for example, forgetting the kiln is on or being called away just at the wrong moment, are essential there are other alternatives. A kiln sitter cut-off device makes use of ceramic cones. When the selected cone bends, its collapse trips a switch which cuts off power to the elements. Cones of different grades can be used, according to the temperature or heatwork required, and this mechanical system is a reliable alternative where the switching off alone might otherwise be at risk. A kiln sitter is easily fitted, requires no complicated wiring and, like its elaborate hi-tech counterpart, will have earned its own cost in a relatively short time.

The heat fuse is another even simpler device which cuts off current at a predetermined point. When the temperature inside the kiln exceeds the capability of the fuse it blows, isolating the elements. It must be pointed out that this is really intended as a back-up system, simply to safeguard the kiln against the possibility of accidental overfiring. It is *not* intended for controlling individual firing schedules. Where a pyrometer or cone arrangement is used to ascertain temperature the kiln should be controlled manually throughout the firing so that the heat fuse remains intact. However, should the person carrying out the firing be inadvertently distracted at the critical period, a heat fuse will minimise damage to elements, brickwork and possibly contents, depending on the rating of the fuse. As all systems are fallible to some extent, the use of a back-up would seem to make good sense.

You may find it reassuring to know that in a normal kiln using conventional fuel systems, the rate of increase in temperature at the top end of the firing cycle is relatively slow. An absence from duty for five or ten minutes is not going to result in significant over-firing.

MISCELLANEOUS MACHINES

Apart from a kiln and probably a wheel, there is really nothing else absolutely essential to the production of ceramics. One item I could not personally be without, however, is a whirler. Whirlers are sometimes referred to as banding wheels, or bench top wheels and are normally used to support and spin plates or pots to which bands of colour are to be applied. A whirler is also extremely useful for supporting coiled pots or other hand-built pieces so that the item can be turned easily without having to be handled directly. Heavier cast-iron models are possibly the best, but for coiling it hardly matters.

In a workshop or studio where there is likely to be a considerable amount of reclaim, a pugmill will be a useful and sometimes necessary requirement. In essence, it is a large, overgrown mincing machine used either horizontally or vertically. Clay is introduced via a small hopper, using a levered ram to press it down on to a wormgear. This in turn mixes the clay, churning and forcing it down a barrel from which it is extruded at the other end ready for re-use. Such a piece of equipment can add greatly to the overall performance of a school pottery section, but may prove to be superfluous in a well-ordered one-person operation where output is modest and most clay is taken through to the fired state first time around.

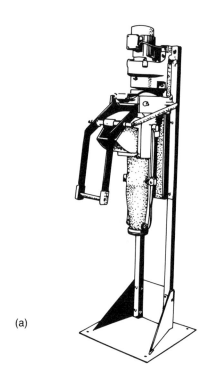

(a)

(b)

Clay is forced through dies of various shapes to produce extruded coils and handle sections. (a) A vertical pugmill. (b) A wadbox.

If any slips or glazes are to be developed and mixed rather than bought in ready-made, scales are essential. For experiments, small but accurate quantities will need to be measured, and a sensitive scale will be necessary. An old, obsolete laboratory scale is excellent for this purpose. When measuring larger batches for general use, a kitchen scale will suffice, or even bathroom scales.

As a workshop becomes established the need for minor items may arise. But bearing in mind both the cost of specialist items and their need for maintenance and storage, it is always worth trying to manage without at first. The person using a spraygun to apply glaze at that pottery you visited last year was probably glazing hundreds of identical items, all with the same glaze. A set of six mugs, on the other hand, could more easily and conveniently be 'dipped' in a bucket, without cost or extensive cleaning up!

TOOLS

The best tools for most ceramic purposes are readily at hand in the form of fingers. The need for others will arise according to the job, and I have tried to indicate such needs where they occur in practical work situations.

Personal Tool Kit

Some tools are essential, both in the preparation process and subsequently to assist in production. Some can be used for a number of different jobs, and it would perhaps be sensible to identify these in order to collect together a 'starter' kit.

Cutting Wire Can be home-made using strong, thin nylon fishing line and two wooden toggles, buttons or pieces of clothes peg. Used for cutting clay when wedging, kneading, preparing balls for throwing and so on. Can be used to cut slabs from blocks of clay. Useful for trimming off uneven rims on thrown wares. Twisted metal wire (*see* diagram below) or nylon is used for removing thrown pots from a wheel.

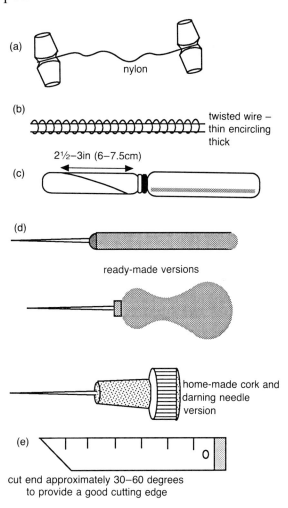

Some potter's tools. (a) Nylon cutter. (b) Twisted wire cutter. (c) Potter's knife. (d) Potter's needles. (e) Dogear tool.

55

Potter's Knife Has a very sharp, tapered point. Its narrow blade does not 'drag' when used to trim plastic clay. Can be purchased or made from a ground-down kitchen or table knife. Used for cutting out slabs, trimming, scoring, piercing and scraping at various stages of the production process.

Sponges Small natural sponges can be purchased from pottery suppliers or, more expensively, as make-up accessories. A small one would be about 2in (5cm) in diameter; larger ones are useful but not essential. Used for cleaning up or 'softening' hard, cut edges and mopping out slurry from thrown wares. Natural is preferable to synthetic which tends to be hard and rather too abrasive; natural sponges also hold more moisture. A large bench sponge is useful for the general cleaning up of wheel and working surfaces; synthetic sponges as used for cleaning cars are ideal.

Potter's Needle Easily made by inserting, eye end in, a darning needle into a wine bottle cork or similar. Bought versions tend to have rather thick needles and thin dowel rod handles which are not so easy to work with, nor so easy to find in clay slurry or water. Used for trimming unevenly thrown rims, for scoring and cutting thin slabs of clay.

Dogear Tool A cut-off 6in (15cm) ruler makes an ideal tool for turning off excess thickness on thrown pots. It is possible to purchase boxwood modelling tools which will do the same job, but they are really too good, and too costly, to be subjected to abrasive contact with revolving clay and wheelhead. Better to make use of a broken ruler or similar, cut and sanded down as shown on page 55.

Metal Kidney Scrapers Made of flexible blued steel. They are relatively cheap to buy so it is not really worth attempting to make your own. One of medium size would suffice. They are used for smoothing and chamfering leatherhard or dry clay wares, they could be used as throwing ribs, and are useful for cutting clay in the absence of a potter's knife. Indispensible for refining the profile shapes of coiled pots, and for cleaning joins in slabbed pieces.

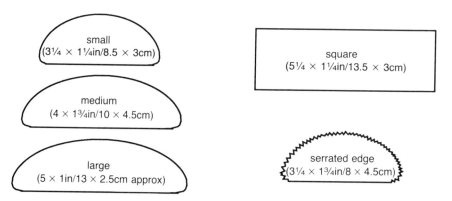

small
(3¼ × 1¼in/8.5 × 3cm)

medium
(4 × 1¾in/10 × 4.5cm)

large
(5 × 1in/13 × 2.5cm approx)

square
(5¼ × 1¼in/13.5 × 3cm)

serrated edge
(3¼ × 1¾in/8 × 4.5cm)

Flexible steel scrapers. Useful, among other things, for smoothing and chamfering leatherhard and dry clay wares.

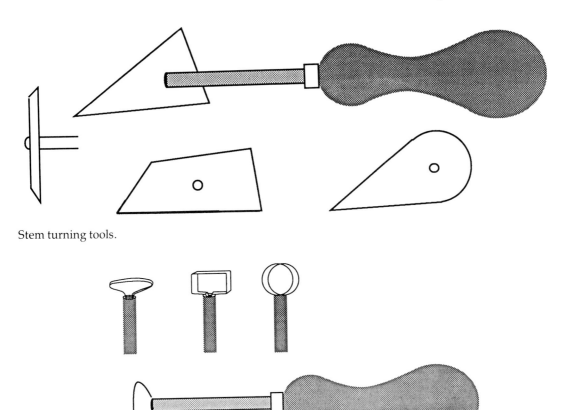

Stem turning tools.

Strip turning tools.

Turning Tools Stem turning tools look rather like paint scrapers, which can often be used in exactly the same way. Strip tools are basically hooped steel cutting tools on stems and handles. They are used for turning.

Metal One-Piece Turning Tools Can be made from hooped iron strips, bent and hardened to provide a variety of cutting edges. Home-made ones sometimes lack rigidity, giving rise to 'chatter'. To make your own you would need a strip of mild steel about 7 × ¾ × ¹⁄₁₂in (18 × 2 × 0.2cm). Cut the end to the profile required (*see* over). Heat the end of the

metal until it is red-hot. Seize it securely in a metal vice and bend to shape – hammer, if necessary. Allow it to cool, then grind or file to produce the desired cutting edges. Various shapes can be made on differing shanks so that a tool will be on hand for almost any turning job.

D.I.Y. Strip Tool Probably the easiest tool to make, and possibly the most useful. For the handle use a piece of planed wood approximately 6 × ¾ × ¼in (15 × 2 × 0.6cm). For the cutting loop use ¼in (0.6cm) blue steel packing strip cut to length and fastened to the handle using

57

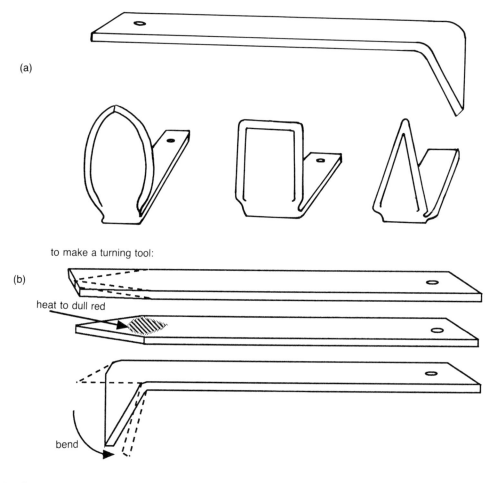

to make a turning tool:

(b)

heat to dull red

bend

(a)   One-piece turning tools provide a variety of cutting edges. (b)   Making a
turning tool.

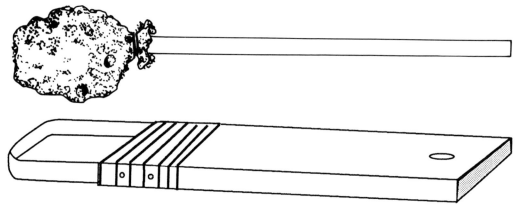

A sponge stick and a D.I.Y. strip tool.

short nails or screws. The join can be covered with plastic tape or whipped with string to ensure that it is secure and that metal ends are safely covered. Metal strip can be bent to any required shape so that a convenient selection of tools can be made. Holes can be bored in handles so that tools can be hung up neatly on a toolboard, using cup hooks or nails.

Sponge Stick Can be purchased, or home-made using a length of dowel rod at the end of which is fastened a piece of sponge, preferably natural. Is used for mopping water or slurry out of the inside of tall and narrow pots during or after throwing.

Modelling Tools A wide range of both boxwood, forged steel, plastic and steel wire looped modelling tools is available from pottery or sculpture suppliers. The better-made versions tend to be expensive, but are much more pleasant to use as well as being more effective. It is probably advisable to obtain just one or two as seems appropriate, improvising somewhat rather than investing in a whole range of items which may be used very infrequently, if at all.

Gather the above items, together with a collection of miscellaneous items such as old forks, a spoon or two, combs, toothbrush, discarded saw blades of varying coarseness and almost anything else you think could be used to impress, scratch, scrape, cut, pat, paddle or otherwise mark or manipulate clay. You will then have an ample tool kit with which to embark upon your ceramics career.

Workshop Tools

The following list comprises a selection of suggested items which will either add to a personal kit or are necessary for the establishment of a workshop. They would not normally be considered the sort of items to be provided by students attending courses in established studios.

Rolling Pin Wooden ones are usually considered to be the best; clay tends not to stick to them to the extent it does with non-porous materials. They are used for rolling clay slabs. Longer ones are most versatile. 20in (51cm) would be good. Kitchen models are usually a little on the short side. Lengths of plastic drainpipe can be used if rigid enough. A towel roller does the job well. 2 or 3in diameter metal pipe lengths could also be used.

Rolling Guides These are wooden laths which determine the thickness of rolled slabs. In pairs, 18–20in (46–51cm) long, of varying sections to provide different thicknesses. Cross-section dimensions could be $1/4 \times 3/4$in (0.6 × 2cm), $1/2 \times 7/8$in (1.2 × 2.2cm), $5/8 \times 15/16$in (1.5 × 2.4cm) so that they could be used on either edge. We restrict guides to only two thicknesses in the college workshop; about $1/4$in (0.6cm) and about $7/16$in (1cm) to avoid confusion. In our own workshop we use whatever comes to hand to provide the required thickness for a particular job.

Mould Frame This can be purchased or made from four lengths of timber approximately 24–30in (61–76cm) × 6 × 1in (× 15 × 2.5cm) plus four right-angle brackets fixed as in the diagram over, which hold the frame's sides and allow

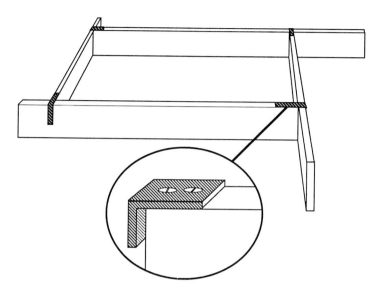

A moulded frame, held together by brackets.

the area containers within to be adjusted as required. The moulded frame is used to cast plaster over a clay plug to make moulds. You can use pieces of timber supported by house bricks or other heavy weights, or a cardboard box of an appropriate size. Seal this with soft clay to prevent leaks.

Harp They are used for cutting slabs from blocks of clay. Various sizes can be purchased. Alternatively, a cutting wire can be used in conjunction with two measured and notched sticks. Strong nylon or steel wire with rings at either end can be stretched taut between the two sticks, with the rings located in appropriate notches to cut the required slab. Both techniques require the use of both hands, and two dowels notched at home are the cheaper!

Sgraffito Tools You can purchase double-ended tools with which to scrape away areas of pigment or slip, or to en-grave or inlay. Potter's knives and needles can be used for the occasional piece, as could almost any sharp tool which can be handled comfortably whilst remaining effective.

Hole Cutters These are available in a range of sizes, and they work like an apple corer, cutting and removing the central core cleanly. Cutters with a semi-circular cross-section clog less than tubular cutters.

Calipers These can be made of wood or plastic, perspex or metal, and are used for checking and comparing measurements, for example when making lids to fit containers. For one-off jobs use either two oil painting brushes held to form a V-shape, adjusted to the measurement to be checked, or one brush or stick held at the required length. (*See* diagram opposite.)

Lawns and Cup Sieves These normally

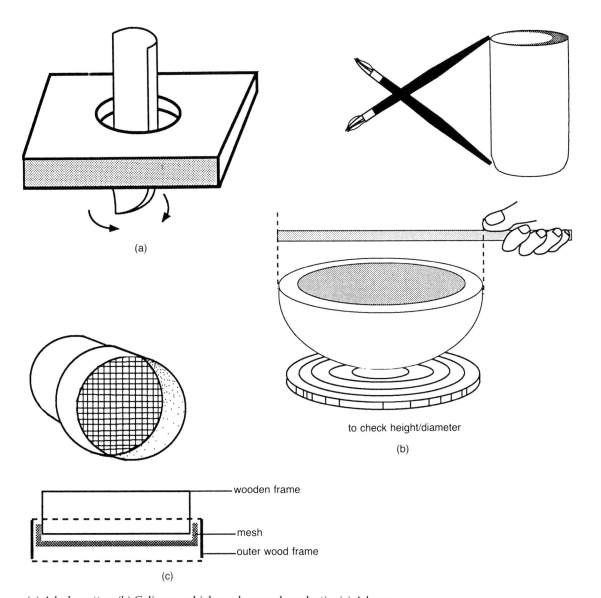

(a) A hole-cutter. (b) Calipers, which can be wood or plastic. (c) A lawn.

have wooden sides with a stainless steel mesh when they are intended for use with working quantitites of glaze or slip. Cup lawns are used for test quantities. Available in meshes from fine 120s to coarse 30s.

Sorting Tools A sorting tool is a cold chisel used for cleaning up kiln furniture and pots after glaze firing. Disused stone or woodcarving chisels can be used, but if it has no tungsten carbide tip it will not be as effective for as long.

Tile Cutters These can be obtained capable of cutting accurate, consistent square, circular or hexagonal tiles from rolled slabs.

Decorating Brushes A wide range of

brushes is available, some for general and others for specific use. My preference is for Japanese brushes which are both versatile in use and beautiful objects in their own right. Two or three different sizes would be sufficient to start with, increasing the range as experience dictates. We also tend to use oil painting and household paint brushes for a multitude of purposes, although when sieving glazes a lawn brush will earn its keep very quickly.

Slip Trailers A slip trailer is usually a soft plastic or rubber bulb fitted with a removable plastic nozzle. Used for trailing slips and/or glazes to decorate. If possible, obtain several so that a range of colours can be used at the same time. They are cheap but not always easy to manage; alternatives come in the form of squeezy bottles.

A quick glance through one of the glossier catalogues provided by suppliers will show the extensive range and variety of tools available to you. It has to be said that having such items to hand can often cultivate and extend the range of personal freedom, technically and aesthetically. Anything that assists in broadening the creative experience has to be considered positively. As an example, perhaps I could mention the clay gun. This useful tool can be used to extrude fine sections of clay. It works rather like a large hyperdermic syringe, without a needle but with interchangeable dies through which clay is forced. Arguably it can be a prop, a gimmick, removing from the student the need to be imaginative or inventive. Similar effects can be obtained by forcing clay through, for example, a kitchen sieve or garlic press. With ingenuity a host of other possibilities will also present themselves. But the tool itself can stimulate ideas and so it could equally be argued that its use is creatively beneficial. The morality of using such tools should therefore not be at issue; however, the cost might be in some instances.

My own preference is for tools which are functional, of minimum cost, require little or no maintenance and have no fiddly but crucial parts which are easily misplaced. When I can achieve the desired end without recourse to tools or equipment I do so. Tools which are multifunctional seem more appropriate to me than those with only a single, and possibly a questionable, use.

The above is not a definitive list, either for personal use or for the setting up of a studio workshop. Personal experience will suggest the need for additional items or for the exclusion of something listed above. What really matters is that you discover for yourself what is right for you, what you feel comfortable using and what you can easily manage without.

6 Techniques for Hand-Building Pots

PINCHING

One of the properties of plastic clay is that it can be pinched and stretched into almost any shape. The simplest way of producing hollow ware is consequently the 'pinching' or 'thumb' method. This has been extensively used to introduce children and adults to the possibilities and 'feel' of clay and unfortunately is often considered by them to be lacking in ceramic dignity. Chances are it has not been introduced in a positive way, and to that extent at least it may have been undersold. Potters throughout the world have produced exquisite forms, both decorative and utilitarian, and the ranks of contemporary artists including craftspeople who have no need of a potters wheel, preferring instead to explore the possibilities of this simple technique to the full, are growing. The beginner will benefit from such close, intimate contact with the material, and will better realise its character and potential.

You should restrict work to palm-sized pots, and to do this you need only enough clay to make a golf-ball sized lump. Place the ball of clay in the palm of one hand, and while turning the clay slowly, gently but firmly press the thumb of the opposite hand into the ball. Work around the clay, opening it up to produce a hollow bowl shape approximately the size of a tennis ball. Gently placing

the soft, newly formed bowl on a firm wooden surface will depress a small foot at its base.

This method is often presented as an introduction to the craft on a first night at evening class, and is dismissed later as an inferior means of producing inferior pots. This is a pity; very refined pieces can be made by the pinching method. Another of the strengths of this technique is that only the simplest tools (hands and fingers) are used. Manual dexterity is developed, together with sensitivity for material and form. Variety of shape and character can be explored, as can simple means of decoration.

When attempting to pinch for the first time it may be found that difficulty is experienced in preventing the vessel from degenerating into a floppy pancake shape. If the rim of the pot is left thicker and narrower than ultimately required the pot will support its form better. A tendency to over-pinch the rim and leave the foot too thick will also be overcome. By concentrating on the middle and lower end of the form it should soon be possible to produce cylindrical or spherical forms.

By joining together several appropriately pinched and pulled or modelled pieces all manner of objects can be produced, from salt cellars and money-box pigs to complex sculptural pieces. Pinch-formed work usually consists of fairly

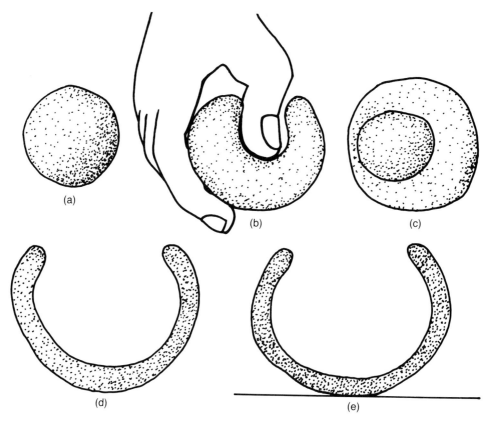

(a) Using a golf ball size lump of clay, pinch it and insert the thumb (b) whilst turning it with the other hand. (c) The plan view shows the hole off-centre. (d) Pinch the shape to even out unequal thickness. (e) The foot can be formed by tapping the bowl on to a firm wooden surface.

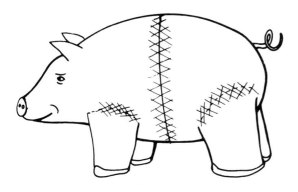

All manner of animal forms can be built up using thumb or pinch pots as prefabricated units. Sound joins must be made – score all surfaces to be joined and apply a liberal coat of slip. Clean the outside by modelling and scraping once the joints have firmed up.

small component parts, so most clays are suitable. A plastic body containing a supportive grog might be better if used by very young children: the adherence and support are both useful where enthusiasm and spontaneity are more in evidence than pure sophisticated craftsmanship.

Joining

The means of joining together two pieces of prefabricated clay is simple and universal. The objective is to weld both bodies together, to obtain a unified join containing no weaknesses to cause prob-

(a)

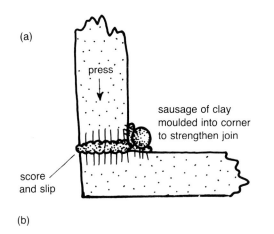

press

sausage of clay moulded into corner to strengthen join

score and slip

(b)

liquid clay (double cream consistency) made from same clay as pieces to be joined

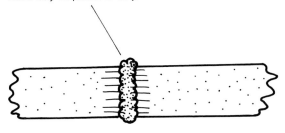

Joining slabs. Press and 'jiggle' slabs together, squeezing out excess slip. The join can be scraped clean later.

lems later. As the same technique is used for practically every joining contingency let us go through it carefully, step by step.

1   Both bodies to be joined must be, as near as possible, the same consistency; in other words, one should not be stiffer than the other. Ideally they should both be *leatherhard*.
2   Both surfaces should be well scored (roughened-up) where contact is to be made.
3   Both surfaces should be liberally coated with slip (*see* Glossary).

4   Surfaces should be brought into contact with each other with firm pressure so that excess moisture, or air, can be excluded.
5   Clean off with a damp sponge.
6   If possible support corner joints (*see* Slabbing page 88) with coils of clay modelled into joints.
7   When the object has stiffened to leatherhardness (*see* Glossary, page 185), outsides of joins can be scraped with an appropriate tool.

SLABBING

Clay can be squeezed and rolled out into flat, uniformly thick slabs which can then be formed, and cut and pressed in various ways. Having prepared the clay ready for use there are two ways that flat slabs can be made.

A lump of clay can be cut into slices using a harp with a wire which can be moved in equal degrees to vary the height of the cut. A harp can be used effectively to cut bagged clay which has been permitted to stiffen up too much for throwing, either for recycle or, more constructively, to pre-fabricate rectilinear forms or whatever else the clay is still capable of. When using relatively soft clay harp-cut slabs can be somewhat difficult to handle without some sort of support.

The second method is to pat (often interpreted as bang or bash) and roll the clay using a rolling pin, laths to determine thickness, and a sheet of canvas upon which the clay will be rolled out. First reduce the overall thickness of the lump of clay. This can be done by constantly throwing it down on to the canvas, turning top to bottom at each throw.

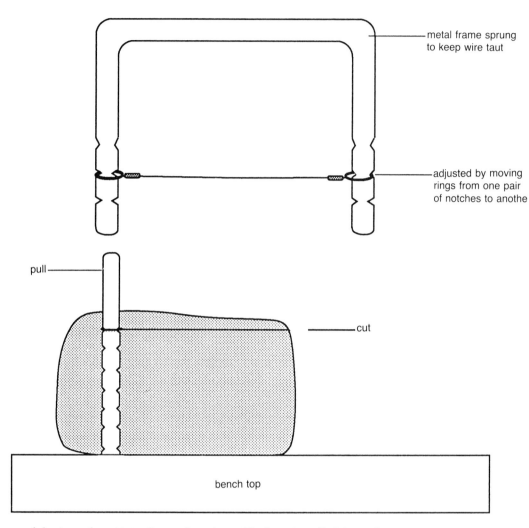

metal frame sprung to keep wire taut

adjusted by moving rings from one pair of notches to anothe

pull

cut

bench top

A lump of clay is easily cut into slices using a harp. The harp is pulled through like a cheese cutter, slicing the clay into slabs of uniform thickness, starting at the top. The harp must be kept as near to vertical as possible.

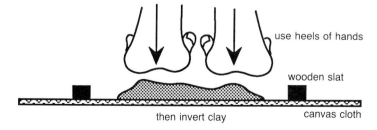

use heels of hands

wooden slat

canvas cloth

then invert clay

Hand-press clay into a rough slab about 1in (2.5cm) thick.

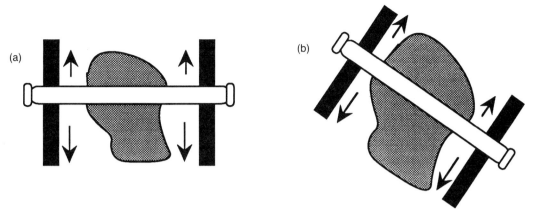

The pat and roll method. (a) Start in the middle, rolling outwards, reducing thickness a little at a time. (b) Move laths-slats and roll to stretch clay diagonally. Turn clay over to release it from the canvas, making it easier to roll out.

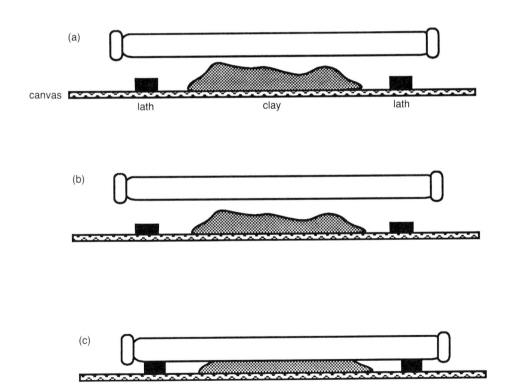

Repeat rolling and turning until the rolling pin can be heard contacting the laths. The slab will then be the same thickness as the laths.

Flatten by hand on to a canvas sheet.

Turn frequently to encourage stretching and avoid sticking.

Roll from the middle outwards, using laths as guides to thickness.

Alternatively the lump can be patted or punched down using the heels of the hands, and again turning regularly. The turning prevents one-sided stretching and adherence to the cloth, which inhibits stretching in any case.

When the clay has been reduced to a more reasonable thickness of perhaps about 1in (2.5cm) or so, it can be rolled. Turning regularly will again permit stretching of the clay and make the job quicker and easier. Use the rolling pin in different directions too, to avoid excessive effort or uneven distribution of the mass. Place the laths at either side of the clay, within the overall lengths of the rolling pin so that when the pin is rolling on the wooden lath the clay will get no thinner. The laths are not intended as a means of obtaining straight edges to the slabs; they will be cut to size as required later.

Making use of the 'original situation' scenario mentioned earlier (the pebble and hole idea), there are in fact two possible ways a slab could be converted simply into some sort of dish. By carefully pressing it into the hollow left by the stone a primitive press-moulded dish can be formed, in what is effectively a 'female' mould.

Gently ease into the mould.

Roughly trim to size.

A rubber kidney is used to smooth the clay in.

Use a ruler or guide lath to level off the rim.

Project–Make a Pebble Dish

The pebble itself could alternatively be used as a male mould, over which the slab might be draped, trimmed prior to careful removal. It may be found that the pebble selected is causing clay to stick to it due to a rough surface texture. Try coating it with slip, or a mixture of slip and liquid soap, to seal the surface. Cling-film would do the job equally well. Do not leave the clay to dry out completely before removing it. It might then be impossible to remove and will be less easy to trim and clean up.

An indentation in the ground is not the most convenient mould to use at the best of times, so contemporary potters use portable holes or depressions cast or carved into blocks of plaster of Paris. These have the advantage of being porous. This speeds up the drying of the clay once it is pressed into the mould, and the dish is still protected and supported in its new shape. Similarly, a male mould cast in plaster will give support and convenient guidance for trimming the slab to shape. Both can be used time and time again to repeat the basic form, which can then be decorated.

(a)

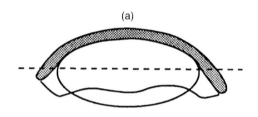

(b)

(c)

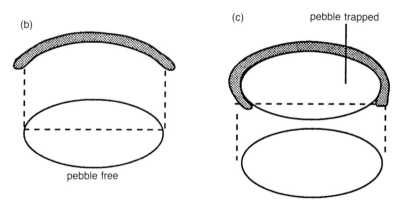

Making a pebble dish. (a) Trim off excess clay at or above the widest point so that the pebble is not trapped by an overhang. (b) A good result – the pebble can freely be removed. (c) When the pebble is trapped, the clay will split as it shrinks around the pebble.

Soften edge with wet fingers or a sponge.

Paper stencils can be used to decorate a pot.

White slip being applied.

Removing paper stencils. Leaves could be used instead.

Project – Make a Press-Mould for Production of Dishes

Plaster of Paris

Use either plaster of Paris, fine dental plaster or potter's plaster. To mix:

Always add plaster to water. 5–6lb plaster to 3 pints of water (2.2–2.7kg to 1.7l) depending on type of plaster used. Put sufficient water in a suitable container. Plaster should be sprinkled on to the water a little at a time, allowing it to sink at its own rate. Where it is intended to carve the mould it is best to dry-sieve the plaster as it is added to the water. When the required amount has been added, stir the mix by hand, feeling for possible lumps and squeezing out if necessary to obtain an even consistency. Pour steadily, but quickly, into the mould (*see* page 79) so that the plug and shuttering are not disturbed.

Tapping or vibrating of the mould immediately after pouring will bring air bubbles to the surface and ensure that plaster has flowed into all corners (or complex undercuts if casting a modelled figure, for example). Clean your mixing receptacles before the plaster sets. 'Kill' wet plaster with running water.

Always remember that plaster must never be allowed to contaminate clay.

On a suitable board model a solid plug of the same dimensions as the required depression then follow the instructions

Pebble 'plug' coated with slip.

Plug lowered into semi-set plaster, with locating keys pressed in.

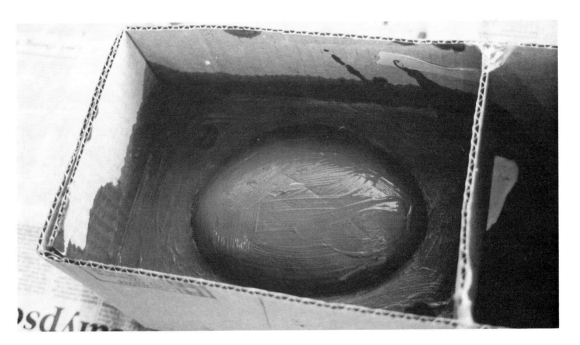

Ready for second layer of plaster. Plaster and plug coated with slip to aid release.

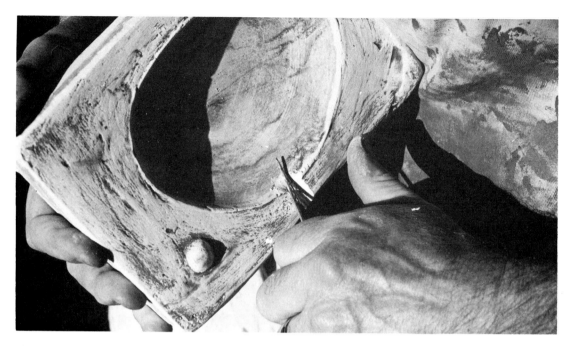

Mould separated: cutting a pouring hole which will form a spout.

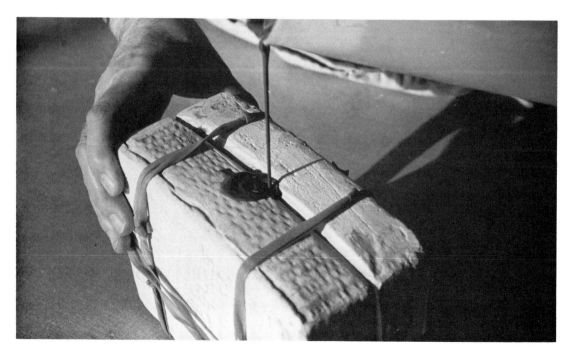

Filling with slip made from own-dug clay.

Invert to drain off excess slip.

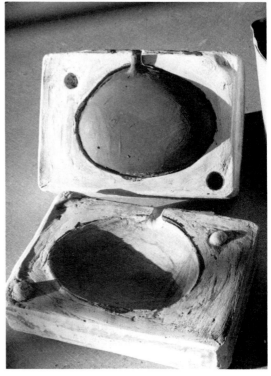

Carefully separate moulds to reveal pot *in situ.*

The pot is removed from the moulds.

given in the illustration over to construct your press-mould. When the plaster has set hard (in about thirty minutes), remove bricks and wooden retaining walls. Check to see if the plaster block can be moved off the base-board (this is not very likely). Carefully invert, so that the base-board is now a lid. By gentle tapping and easing the board will eventually lift off revealing the block of clay inside the plaster. This can now be carefully removed. Do not use metal tools, which could scratch or chip the plaster. With luck the clay will come out clean, with no plaster scraps attached. If it is contaminated by the plaster either keep it separate for modelling use only, or get rid of it.

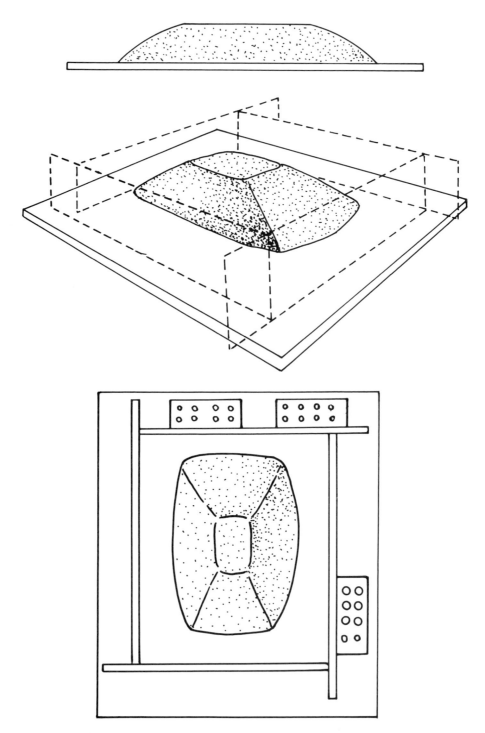

Making a press-mould for the production of dishes. Arrange shuttering as indicated, allowing a minimum of 1in (2.5cm) borders. Seal all joints with plastic clay to prevent leakage. Use building bricks or similarly heavy blocks to support the walls.

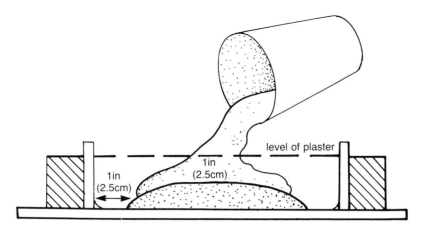

Fill the inside with plaster of Paris to cover the plug by 1in (2.5cm) at its highest point.

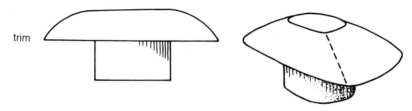

A male mould, over which a clay slab is laid, stretched to conform and then trimmed flush.

You are left with a dish-shaped hole in a lump of plaster which requires thorough drying out, preferably on top of a kiln, for several days, and will also need trimming. Sharp edges and corners should be carved away from the outer edges of the mould, preventing possible chipping and clay contamination later. This is best done before the mould is dried out, after which it becomes hard and brittle, and not at all easy to tidy up.

Instead of using the neat professional method outlined above, the same end can be realised by first making the plug on a cling-film or plastic-covered base. This will allow the plug to be lifted off the board and lowered into place on the bottom of a suitably sized cardboard box. Provided the box does not leak, all that then need be done is to cover the plug with plaster. Bricks supporting the outside of the box will go some way to prevent it sagging, and once the plaster sets the cardboard can be torn off, clay removed and all edges and corners trimmed as above. The end result is not such a neat, tidy mould but it will obviously work just as well as its professional counterpart, and requires less in the way of equipment.

A male mould, cast in plaster, can also be used. The clay slab is laid over the mould, carefully stretched to conform, and trimmed flush. The disadvantage of this method is that the inside of the dish cannot be decorated until removed from the mould. It also eliminates slip-trailing, unless this is carried out before the slab is laid on.

Project – Make a Two-Section Moulded Form

Before discussing uses for flat slabs of clay cut and assembled to produce recti-linear (box) structures, it ought to be mentioned that the use of some form of mould with which to pre-form clay is not confined to the production of dishes. Us-ing a symmetrical dish mould, two pieces can be produced which can be directly joined together to form the belly of a pot or sculptural piece. Necks, spouts and handles could be added for decorative or functional purposes. Decoration poss-ibilities are endless, exploring texture and pattern on broad surfaces begging to have something exciting done to them.

The two basic pieces could be joined by a layer or two of coils or sausages of clay rolled out and used to build up a stouter form. The easiest way to do this is to make the first section, allowing it to stif-fen somewhat, remove it from the mould and store it safely, well wrapped so that it cannot become too dry. Having pres-sed in a second half, allow it to stiffen to the same extent in the mould, and then, whilst it is supported by the plaster, build up the extending wall to make the join between the two.

It will not be possible to model in the last join unless part of the form is cut away, so the wiggling and pressing at this last stage are rather important. The aim is to get a good, solid join in the clay so scoring and a liberal application of 'double cream' thickness slip must not be scrimped.

Again this belly form can be used in numerous ways, the only restrictions being the imagination of the maker, and the need to make at least one small hole in the form to prevent it exploding when

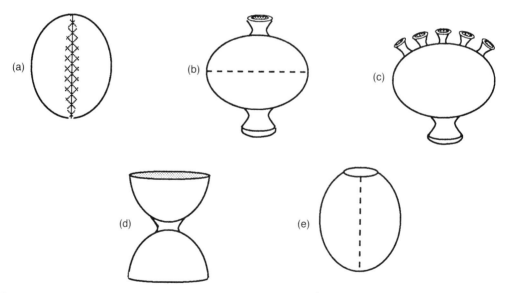

Making a two-section moulded form. (a) Two dish forms joined (scored and slipped) to make belly. (b) and (c) They can then be fitted with thrown necks, feet or other appendages. (d) The form could be cut and rejoined. (e) The foot can be formed by gentle paddling or bumping when leatherhard, or cut and fitted with a slabbed foot. The top can be cut off to make a vase.

heated in the kiln. Air expands upon heating and if it cannot escape via a spout or neck it will cause the object to break, usually at a weak point such as a join or thin section.

All manner of means can be used to pre-form clay either into simple dished forms or as sections to be assembled into some larger piece. Clay can be supported in 'hammocks' or shaped over any suitable 'male' type humps. Imagination and ingenuity can be applied to the full, the only restrictions being over or undercuts, shrinking and drying, all of which (as in most ceramic production) should be carefully controlled or avoided.

To sum up, clay can be preformed; supported in or on some sort of form often made of plaster of Paris. Any other material can be used, provided it releases the clay. Highly glossy non-absorbent surfaces are not usually suitable because as the clay stiffens, it shrinks. If it is stuck fast to a supporting surface tension builds up to the point that the clay will

crack. The same is true if clay is wrapped around an overhang. An extreme example might be a bottle wrapped in clay. As the moist clay becomes drier it shrinks and actually increases its grip on the non-shrinking bottle until the clay breaks. When a single unit, such as a dish, is required it is possible to leave the clay *in situ* until completely dry. Where sections are to be prefabricated for later assembly it is essential that the clay must not dry out. It has to be stiffened to leatherhard so that it can be removed, wrapped up, and stored until required. In a leatherhard state the clay should have the consistency of Cheddar cheese. It should be easily cut (without the material sticking to the tool), malleable enough to allow some bending, and plastic enough to allow good solid joins to be made. Reference will be made again to the state of the clay because it is when clay is about the hardness of cheese that it can most easily be joined, while sufficiently firm to retain its desired shape.

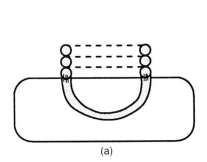
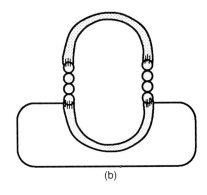

(a) (b)

Joining using coils. (a) Model the ropes or coils of clay together. Score the rim of the dish and add slip to ensure adequate adhesion to the stiffer clay.
(b) Carefully position the first dish on top of the extending coils, having scored its rim and added a coating of slip. Press and wiggle it firmly down to exclude air and excess slip which will ooze out at the joint. The coils used to form the extending wall should be welded together on the inside prior to closing up the form. Smoothing on the outside is best carried out when the join has been allowed to stiffen up a little more.

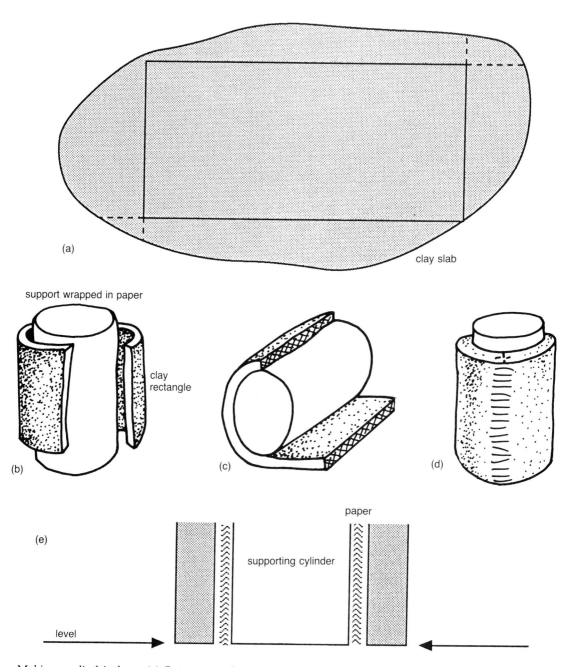

Making a cylindrical pot. (a) Cut a rectangle to make best use of the slab. (b) Score and slip both surfaces to be joined and bring them firmly together. (c) Pick up slab by rolling it on to a supporting cylinder. (d) Weld and smooth surface join thoroughly. This should be a good join as the inside may not be accessible to weld. (e) Check that no paper is protruding at the join – trim if necessary.

Project – Make a Simple Cylindrical Pot

1   Roll a slab of clay.
2   Allowing the size of slab to dictate the size of vessel, cut a rectangle from the slab long enough to wrap around a selected support (for example a bottle, a rolling pin, a piece of plastic pipe).
3   Wrap the supporting cylinder with old newspaper to prevent the slab sticking to its support.
4   Wrap the supporting slab around its support to form a clay cylinder.
5   Gently tap both support and clay to slide the clay cylinder to level with the bottom of its support.
6   With luck there will be a piece of original slab remaining that is big enough to use for a base.
7   Use a plywood board or batt as a base board.
8   Score the surface to be joined, apply slip, and bring them into contact.
9   Trim off any excess clay from the base using a potter's knife.
10   It is useful to leave about a ¼in (0.6cm) foot protruding, so that clay from the base can be modelled upward. Use a finger or modelling tool to weld the base up into the tube and neaten.
11   It may now be necessary to trim the top rim of the cylinder, as the clay may have stretched and distorted during building.
12   In addition to the base-board I always build pieces on a bench whirler or banding wheel. This makes it easier to revolve work without actually handling it, and avoids accidental damage.

When rolling out slabs of clay for a specific job you will find that it is advisable to roll out one or two extra so that if an

Gently lift cylinder, using both hands and with the support still inside, and lower it firmly into place on to the slab which will form the base. Use a potter's knife to trim off excess clay.

Use a modelling tool to weld the join between foot and wall, working the clay smoothly upwards. Gently loosen and remove the internal support.

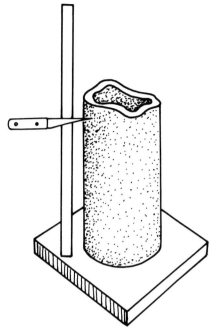

A stick or ruler with knife or pencil can be used to prick or score around at the required height.

accident befalls one section you will have a replacement at hand in the same leather-hard state as the original. After successfully completing the project there will probably be surplus slab left over. After taking the time and trouble to make them it would be a pity to waste the off-cuts. So consider what else could be made with them, rather than simply recycling.

Project – Making Box Forms

Making use of any off-cuts available, make a square or rectangular ash or peanut tray (see diagram below).

Pattern Making

When making any form of slabbed pot, and taking advantage of some of the

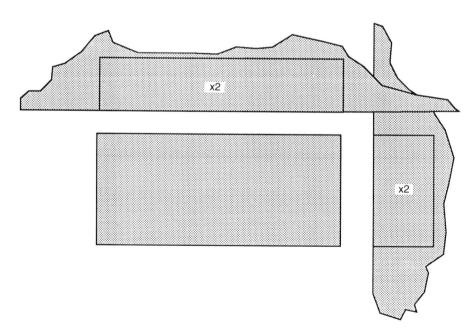

Making a box form. Use odd offcut pieces of slab for the walls and base. The base size will be determined by the size of the spare slabs available. When marking out, remember to take into account the thickness of the slabs.

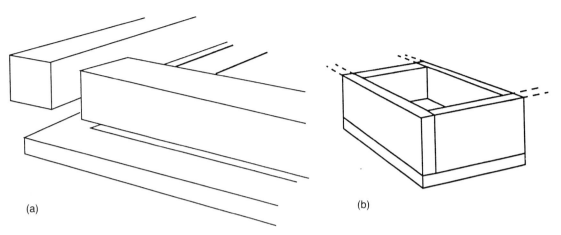

(a) Score all surfaces to be joined and apply slip. (b) The completed box – either use an insert join or lapped corners (as in the adjustable mould-making frame).

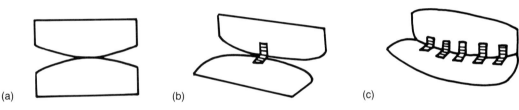

Pattern making is useful to test the practicality of your ideas. (a) Two curved edges to be joined. (b) Lay the pieces flat and join with a small piece of tape in the centre of the curve. (c) Ease into shape, taping outwards from the centre. The taped join pulls flat 'slabs' into curved surfaces. When making patterns in card, keep the curves subtle and understated.

material's characteristics, it is tempting to oversimplify the process and neglect other methods. Slabbing can be regarded as a mixture of dressmaking and joinery methods. Working from a design, a paper pattern can be cut out as a guide. Slabs are then cut mechanically to conform to the pattern, and assembled. However, two aspects of this are worth considering. Patterns can make the assembly easier and also offer a means of testing the design.

A major aim of the design process is to produce an object with a pleasing and acceptable appearance overall. It should also effectively fulfil expectations of function. In other words, your project should look good, and work. All this is fine on paper but if the design concept exceeds the capabilities of maker or material it will fall somewhat flat. So a pattern, cut out of medium card, is a useful means of testing the 'makeability' of the design. Pieces should be assembled using adhesive tape at intervals along joins. Taping fully, particularly on curved edges, will not be easy, and is in any event unnecessary.

Reference has been made to design elsewhere (*see* Chapter 3). Suffice to say that if the model is difficult or even impossible to construct using paper or card, it will prove equally difficult, and hence inappropriate, when attempted in clay.

Working to a pattern can be helpful, but developing a sense of 'correctness', the ability to reconcile aims and means, and responsiveness to changing possibilities, are likely to be more useful. By utilising scraps you can play your way into the design and make process without being inhibited by a misplaced concern for 'spoiling' slabs. Neither will you feel confined or restricted by designs which, although they should not do so, often appear difficult to modify, much more so to give up on. The 'playing' approach liberates the maker, so that alternatives are recognised, more interesting formats considered and ultimately a much more mature, considered and acceptable result will be achieved.

One of the merits of using card patterns is that if the designed form proves difficult to construct it can be easily altered. Card, scissors and adhesive tape are arguably more convenient when trying out variations on a basic theme. Discarded patterns can be replaced much more easily than evenly rolled out slabs of leatherhard clay. A wide range of possibilities can thereby be explored using only two or three disposable models. A tall, narrow version could be compared to a short but stable form, and to another somewhere between the two.

Once something approaching the acceptable has been identified, the pattern can be used to mark out basic shapes of slabs. These can be further refined in subtle ways by trimming prior to assembly. By using patterns to aid assembly

and to test the design it is thus possible to combine both the theoretical drawing-board approach and the 'play your way in' approach.

There is no reason why a piece constructed in this way should not be both well-designed in a formal sense, and have qualities of spontaneity, liveliness or contemplative peace, rather than conforming to the sterile stereotype of the machine-age artefact. Your intention should be to produce an article which is interesting to look at and to touch.

Assuming that a basic rectangle 8 × 10in (20 × 25cm) would be a suitable base for an open box construction, roll out a slab. It will roll out into an organic and arbitrary shape. Attempt to mark out an 8 × 10in (20 × 25cm) rectangle.

1 Making best use of space, obtain the required area.
2 If this results in vast areas of excess, use the remainder for something else.
3 *Or* consider larger base, possibly different proportion.
4 *Or* compare length to diameter of available support, and make a cylinder instead!

Shrinkage before and during firing can cause warping to flat, open forms. This can be designed out to some extent by using grogged bodies containing refractory materials which will not shrink any further. A smooth red clay will be less stable in this respect than a coarse-grogged grey clay. If you are a student with no control over choice of the body used by the class you have joined you will have to work accordingly. If on the other hand you are responsible for the provision of clay for student or personal use, it may be worth considering what standard clay body should be provided with regard for the abilities and aspirations of the clients.

Enjoy the processes and do not allow a preconceived notion of what you want spoil the experience.

Project – Make a Lidded Box

1   Design the box form, i.e. square, rectangle, elegant, etc.
2   Assemble on a wooden base-board.

3   If the box is vertically rectangular, assembly on its side may be easier.
4   Ensure that slabs are firmly leather-hard so that they will not sag when assembled.
5   After scoring and brushing slip on to the final slab, supported by a board, carefully invert the box on to the lid so that its own weight aids adhesion.
6   Make the lid by carefully cutting through the walls at the required level, releasing a section of the cuboid. Use a

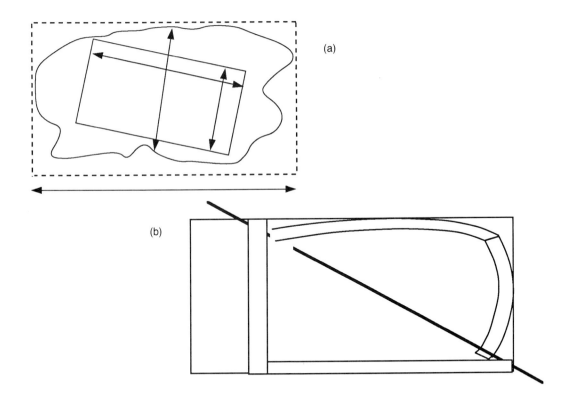

(a)

(b)

Making a lidded box. (a) From a rolled out slab with an overall size of about 12 × 16in (31 × 41cm) it is only possible to cut out a rectangle 7 × 10in (18 × 25cm). (b) Try setting up curved sides to the rectangle, bending walls to the extent of their thickness on length and half their thickness for the width to add a subtle curve. The result may be a more visually interesting shape. A simple arbitrary approach such as this can be used to introduce interest, subtlety and tension. Also, minor distortions in drying and/or firing will be less noticeable in an organic form.

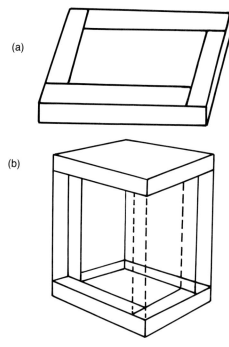

(a)

(b)

(a) The arrangement of the slabs of a lidded box taking into account their thickness.
(b) The overlap system of setting walls.

During the assembly process score and slip all surfaces to be joined. Model a thin sausage into the inside corners to strengthen them. Do not worry about the outside of the box at this stage.

potter's knife to make the cut, working through the wall carefully in stages to avoid over-stressing the clay and possible breakage as a result. If the cut is made at an angle through the wall, inclined inwards, an even more precise fit will be achieved; the lid will only fit in one position, and will not slide off as would be the case with either a plain slab-lid or a lid with horizontal separation cuts.

7 Check that walls are not beginning to concave. There is a tendency during the slabbing of rectilinear forms for the walls to sag in towards the centre, particularly on larger, open forms unsupported by a top slab. Any sagging should be very carefully coaxed out before the clay stiffens to much.

8 Replace lid, check fit and clean up the cut.

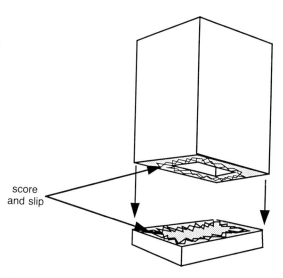

score and slip

Press the constructed box firmly on to its lid, taking care to exclude air and surplus slip. Wiggle it a little to squeeze and weld the lid to the box.

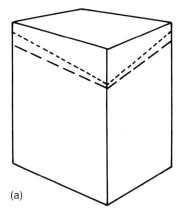
(a)

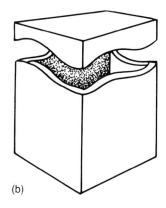
(b)

A variety of lid shapes can be cut. (a) Lid released along a straight but sloping line. (b) An undulating lid. Either will ensure a better fit than straight across. An inclined cut will also assist precise location of the lid.

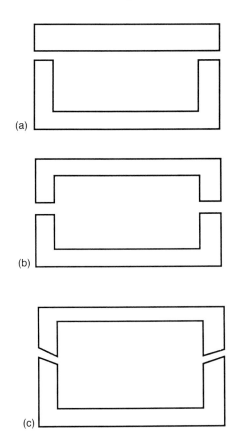

(a)

(b)

(c)

(a) There is nothing to secure this lid.
(b) This lid is also not very secure. (c) An inclined cut prevents the lid sliding sideways. Inward and outward slopes are equally effective.

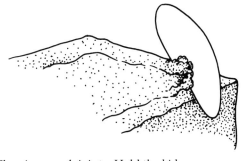

Cleaning rough joints. Hold the kidney scraper at right-angles to the surface. Work diagonally across the joins and inward from the edges and corners to prevent damage.

9 Now examine the outside. Any rough joins can be scraped clean, working diagonally inward from edges to prevent damage, using a straight-edged tool such as a metal kidney scraper (*see* diagram above).

10 When the scraping has been completed, the outside of the box will look clean and flat, with sharp, square edges. These can be rounded off by rubbing them gently with a dry thumb, or a damp sponge. This will soften the edges, making them more agreeable to the eye and to touch. The rounded-off edges will more readily accept glaze, so that a uniform covering will be more likely.

COILING

There seems to be the belief among some students I come across that as a method, coiling is either childish or primitive, and not really legitimate pottery. This is in direct contradiciton to the history of the craft over several thousands of years. The fact is that coiling offers an ideal method of hand-building cylindrical vessels without recourse to wheel technology. Its considered building approach provides a unique control over both the material and the form of the pot, which lends itself particularly well to the production of larger, often one-off, pieces. These can be purely functional as in the amphorae of Greece or contemporary garden pots. Alternatively, they can be sculptural, retaining or rejecting identity as a vessel, becoming almost ritualistic.

If your aim is to produce even a limited run of perhaps a dozen mugs or jugs, coiling is not the appropriate method to choose. Equally, it is difficult to see how the Chinese warriors could have been thrown on a potter's wheel. There is an obvious truth that some things should, and must, be made on a wheel. Other things can only be made by other means.

There is little profit in attempting to utilise a means which is inappropriate or incapable of producing the desired end; one of the basic skills required by the would-be potter is the ability to select an appropriate method of working to fulfil a given intention, or conversely to identify an appropriate goal to be met via a given method. The same is true when seeking a solution to any design problem; it is all too often the case that design possibilities are lost due to the restrictive nature of an arbitrarily chosen material or means of production.

Coil Construction

The merits of coil construction are several. Like slabbing, it is methodical. The object under construction grows by being deliberately built layer by layer, either rising vertically from its foot or swelling as coils are made of larger diameter, and reducing when the size of each is restricted again. The profile is carefully determined, together with proportion and size, by adjusting the size of coils, and later by paddling or patting the form, from inside as well as out.

When throwing pots on a wheel, slabbing, or even slip-casting, size will be significantly restricted by limitations of wheel power, size of rolling pin, your body strength, and so on. Given an appropriate clay body there is really no restriction to the size of a coiled pot. In fact this method is particularly suited to the production of really large pots. Beginners will perhaps be restricted by their skill and ability to recognise the condition of the clay and its capability to maintain the form whilst still remaining wet enough to be rolled out and moulded together. They are tempted to progress too quickly, building height before lower layers can support the excessive weight, not yet realising that sometimes more can be achieved by letting the lower layers of clay stiffen before adding too much weight to upper parts, particularly where it is intended to build in dramatic changes of direction.

Constructional problems will quickly be overcome with practice, and whereas most people recognise that skills are required before attempts to make pots on a wheel are successful, there is a tendency to believe that coiling will be different. To some extent this is justified. Coil building

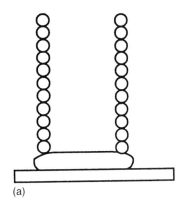
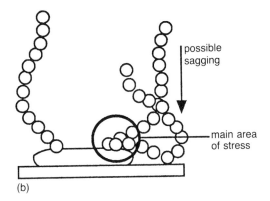

(a)

(b)

Coiling. (a) Vertical walls are capable of supporting a considerable weight of clay. (b) When walls are curved, they are likely to collapse under the weight of clay above. The stress area needs to be allowed to stiffen a little. Size of pot should only be increased as the walls become capable of supporting the extra weight.

calls for fewer manipulative skills, but without care and thought the end result can still be poor. The finished article will reflect the amount of tender loving care lavished or otherwise on the growing form and the character of the maker. Your aim should be to produce a well-proportioned pot, stimulating to eye and touch, and possibly useful at the same time. If you manage this at the very first attempt you should consider yourself favoured. It is likely that several attempts will usually be required before you feel confident with the process.

Before looking at the building process you must acquire the knack of producing coils of clay made uniformly in an appropriate thickness. Hand rolling is the traditional method, and it has several advantages. It requires no machinery, and can be done on virtually any flat worksurface. If any difficulties are experienced when attempting to make coils the chances are that the clay is not in the right condition. It is a basic fact of a potter's life that clay must always be in

the correct condition for its required use. Attempting to roll out clay which is too wet will cause it to adhere to everything; clay which is a little too hard will not roll out readily or evenly. Some potters prefer to work with a slightly stiffer body than would be used for throwing because they consider it more self-supportive once it is *in situ*. As a general guide, I would suggest that if you can knead it then you can coil it, so have a try.

Your aim is to produce rope-like lengths of clay of an even thickness and with a round cross-section. Work on a dry, slightly absorbent surface such as a plain wooden board. Prior to rolling it is a good idea to squeeze the lump of clay, using both hands alternately, turning whilst squeezing. The result will be a thick short sausage of clay perhaps 1½in (4cm) thick which will then require rolling to stretch it into a longer, thinner coil. If you are unable to close thumb and forefinger around the sausage it will probably still be too thick to roll easily.

Place the thick sausage on the work

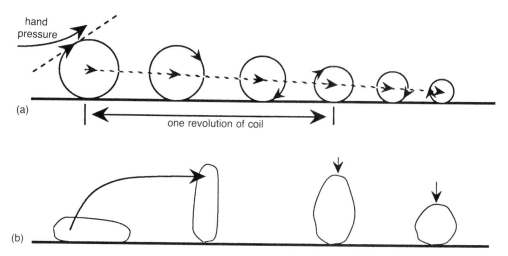

Coil construction. (a) Allow the coil to 'run'. Too much downward pressure will flatten the coil, as will not rolling for a full revolution. (b) If a coil is not perfect, stand it on its end and tap down on its top, then re-roll the coil. In this situation it may also help to twist the coil lengthwise and roll again.

Squeezing a rope before rolling into a coil.

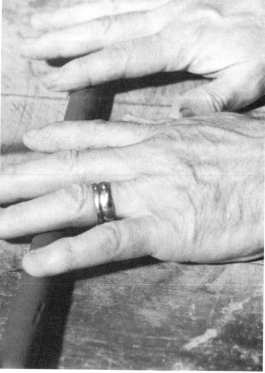

Rolling out a coil.

surface so that it can be rolled away from you, using both hands. Apply enough downward pressure to extend the clay sideways a little, and coax it to roll easily. When the clay is beneath your hands reapply fingers so that the heels of the hands release and the clay rolls further away than would have been the case using a single hand span. The coil should complete at least one revolution, and if possible should be allowed to run for several. In this way the cross-section will be round; shorter runs will produce flattened, oval coils which are much more difficult to build together.

Bring the coil back to original position and repeat as necessary to obtain the correct thickness. The old adage 'little and often' applies here, as in numerous other ceramics situations. Do not try to achieve too much at each movement. Your material has taken millions of years to become clay and does not appreciate being rushed into new states and shapes. With a little practice your coils will be easy to produce, and satisfying to use, aiding you in your quest for a well-constructed piece.

One of the advantages of hand-rolling coils is that the condition of the clay is confirmed, or not as the case may be. It heightens tactile appreciation of the material and what can be done with it. There are other advantages too. Each coil can be rolled as required, avoiding the production of a large number in advance only to find that some if not all of them have dried and stiffened up too much before they are required for use. Time spent rolling the next coil gives previously applied clay a little chance to dry *in situ*, to some extent promoting the stiffening process necessary to support the weight of added height, and stresses

to the structure arising from exaggerated deviations from the vertical, as illustrated in the drawing on page 91.

Before describing more fully the way to tackle coil-building there are a few tips of a general nature which should be born in mind as you work through the process.

1 It is best to make individual, single coils or circles of clay, rather than one long coil. The former will give more precise control over the growth of the vessel; each can be placed exactly in place, and made to a size which follows the eventual shape of the vessel.

2 Each coil should be modelled in to the previous one, or the base, on the *inside* only, as it is put in place. Do not build up the form and then attempt to reach down inside it. This will almost certainly cause leaning or sagging of the pot.

3 Depending on the size of vessel, and whether you are working constantly on the building, or constructing it over a period of time, do *not* model together coils on the outside until the clay has stiffened up to a soft leatherhard. This will allow the pot to consolidate its form without undue pressures being applied which might distort it.

4 Lower coils on large pots should be modelled together before they have dried too much, constructing upper layers as per 3 above.

5 If work is to be carried over until another day make sure that the pot is adequately protected against premature drying. Put a plastic bag over it, exclude as much air as possible and close it up tightly at the foot. Gently tucking the plastic slightly under the base makes for a good seal.

6 When applying a fresh coil to a section stored as above for any length of

time, check the old clay for stiffening. If its consistency is even slightly firmer than the fresh clay it is advisable to score the old coil and apply slip before adding a new coil. Ensure that the slip is thick; do *not* add water. This could cause the pot to become soggy and prevents the desirable controlled drying process.

7 To model one coil into another, use either a finger, thumb or modelling tool. Do *not* use water, with or without sponge.

To sum up, work steadily, concentrating on the *internal* shape first, and avoid the use of free water.

Project – Build a Coil Pot based on a Cylinder

The finished work should have parallel, straight sides. Try to identify a 'perfect' proportion, height, breadth. Is the cylinder too short, or too tall? Is it to have a function? If so how is its proportion affected?

1 Use a base-board. A square piece of five ply will do. Thin pieces are adversely affected by the damp; they warp and thereby distort pots built upon them. Ideally marine or exterior quality plywood should be used.
2 Make a sphere out of clay. The ball should be about the size of a golf or squash ball.
3 Place on the base-board and gently but firmly depress the centre of the clay, turning clay constantly so that a flat disc is made, about the thickness of a finger. With practice it will soon be possible to make balls which will flatten to form bases of the required size. But remember, you are not working to a micrometer

measurement. Just let the pot grow to fit its base.
4 Roll out a rope or sausage of clay approximately as thick as the finger selected above, i.e. the same thickness as the base.
5 Pinch off an end of the coil.
6 Lower the coil into place to form a vertically circular wall built directly above the base disc so that the cylinder has the same diameter as the base disc.
7 Model into base.
8 Continue adding coils, modelling each into the previous one, until the required height is reached. In profile the cylinder will appear as a rectangle (*see* Chapter 3).

If a bench whirler is available, it will be easy to turn the work frequently to check vertical growth. Pots have a tendency to grow towards the maker if they are not turned frequently. If the profile is checked at forty-five degree intervals, i.e. eight times in one revolution, any slight lean will be noticed in sufficient time to build it out with successive coils.

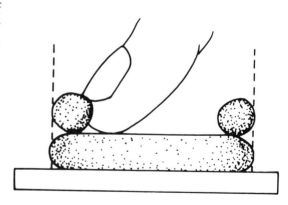

Modelling the first coil on to the base. Use a finger or thumb and work around inside the coil fingerprint by fingerprint to ensure a good weld. Leave the pattern of prints to add interest.

9   As the clay stiffens, the pot will be safer to handle. The outside can now be modelled in, either for eventual smoothing with a metal kidney or by using fingers or modelling tools to create decorative textural patterns resulting from the tooling. Some areas of smoothness can be complimented by areas of pattern so that the coils are joined firmly together and the pot decorated at the same time. Pattern and texture which occur incidental to the process of putting the pot together are arguably the most honest and justifiable forms of decoration. Such decoration frequently has an integrity and appropriateness to the form which self-conscious attempts to reproduce commercially used motifs could never have. Even your first attempt at coiling a pot will be an exciting combination of problems. The satisfaction of producing a successfully constructed vessel will be further enhanced by the experience gained by empirically applying decoration during the building process.

Project – Build a Coil Pot based on a Sphere

The method required to build a sphere is similar to constructing a cylinder. A major difficulty is, of course, to visualise the eventual form and to put coils on to achieve a circular profile, with no awkward changes of direction occurring within the curve.

1   Start with a narrow base about 1–1½in (2.5–4cm) in diameter, and as thick as your little finger.
2   As coils are built up to form the curved wall it will probably be best to slightly understate the curve initially.
3   When modelling together the coils on

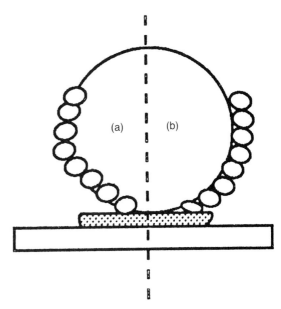

Constructing a coil pot based on a sphere. (a) Coils are placed slightly inside the desired line of profile. (b) After the coils are welded together, the sides will be stretched outward as a result of working on the inside of the form.

the inside of the pot, support the wall outside with the other hand so that the coils are not stretched to a greater diameter than required. Some distortion will inevitably occur so the built-in understatement will now be eased out to the exact profile shape.
4   Remember that there will not be a vertical support upward from the coils below, so do not rush the building. When an open bowl-shape has been reached, i.e. about one quarter of the whole, allow the structure to stiffen a little. To quicken the process make use of sun and breeze, turning the pot frequently to prevent uneven drying. When it is impossible to put pots outside, on cold wet days for example, you can hurry the job along by playing a hair drier over the form.

Base formed from a flattened ball of clay.

The first coil is moulded in

Several coils are now *in situ*.

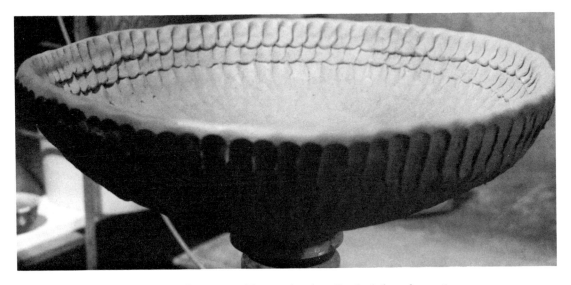

Patterns created by thumbs and fingers working on the clay. Can be left as decoration.

Score and slip before adding coils if pot has
stiffened at all.

Build directly into the required profile form.

Patting or batting to modify form.

Patterns can be flattened and scraped, to
obtain a clean outline and to develop
surface texture.

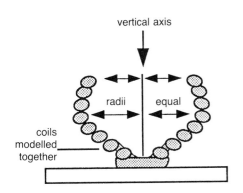
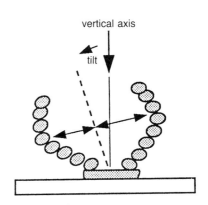

Check the visual profile of the pot. (a) In this cross-section the axes of the coils are vertically centred on the base. (b) In this cross-section the axes of the coils are obviously not centred vertically on the base.

5   At this stage, begin resolving outside coils. Either smooth completely, or perhaps leave textures of tooled pattern.
6   Continue building, checking the profile shape visually and that coils are built to a common vertical axis (*see* diagram above).
7   A ruler or plumb line could be used to check vertical growth but, particularly on large vessels, a rolling pin stood on end inside, centred on the base, can be a very useful guide. Obviously you will not want to leave the rolling pin in position while work is in progress. If it fell over an exaggerated asymmetry would result which would almost certainly be impossible to correct.
8   Work on the internal form, checking constantly the external shape. Using knuckles or a suitable tool, ease the walls outward if necessary, to obtain the desired profile, supporting the wall immediately outside whilst doing so. By this means subtle changes can be made to correct slight deviations arising from the building process, but drastic irregularities will probably not respond without structural damage to the pot. Corrections should be made gently, a little at a time, and with due care it will be found that where necessary even small kinks in the profile can be eased away. Always work upwards, diagonally across coils.
9   If the form is closed in to a narrow neck you will find that a thumb will be the best means of modelling coils internally.
10   As with the cylinder the choice is now to smooth or not to smooth. If tooling patterns have been built up on the surface it may be worth making one smooth coil, modelled to an appropriate shape to complete the overall design and give resolution to the neck or lip of the pot. Similar attention should be given to the foot. A vessel which begins and ends well will not have to rely so heavily on what happens in between for its success. It is worth remembering that potters do not just look at the profile or inside of a pot. An almost reflex reaction is to pick a pot up and examine the foot. This will reveal not only a potter's mark or signature but also the character, both of the pot and to some extent the potter.

If the pot is to be scraped smooth it will be found that a flexible metal kidney tool will take off raised points, using the flat edge of the tool. Work diagonally across the pot, turning all the time to avoid flat areas. Constantly check the profile, taking off thin scrapings of clay until a continuous curve is created, with no high or low spots. Using a kidney tool it is possible to consolidate the profile, thus obliterating the original horizontal pattern of coils or arbitrary pattern and texture resulting from the work put in.

Clay containing aggregates in the form of grog or sand particles will produce exciting scored textures, with occasional pitting, caused by particles of refractory material which have been loosened from the body dragged across the surface. By adjusting the angle or direction of attack, texture can be heightened; by gently tapping with a smooth tool such as a ruler, or lightly burnishing with a broad, shiny metal tool such as a tablespoon, the texture can be modified or even removed. Equally, you can experiment with different scraping tools to create a wide range of textured surfaces which can be used to advantage in conjunction with other decoration techniques as discussed in Chapter 12.

You will already have noticed that it has not been possible to separate methods and techniques conveniently into totally self-contained chapters. In the above paragraphs we have touched on design and decoration when attempting to deal with the techniques of coil building. It will have become obvious that some clays will be more suitable for hand-building purposes than others. It will be seen that when scraped to achieve smooth surfaces, some bodies will in fact become rough. One body will hold a particular shape where another will collapse. Bearing this in mind, appreciating and capitalising on the characteristics of the clay in hand, must be one of the basic preoccupations of a potter. Fortunately, most clay bodies readily available from pottery suppliers will be reasonably versatile, so that whether you are using a smooth red clay or a coarse raku (see Chapter 10) body you should be able to build both a cylinder and a modestly sized sphere without experiencing exaggerated problems.

If we take for granted the ability also to build a cone, then first you have solved the problems of producing basic ceramic shapes, and second you should now be able to build almost any form combining the basic forms as necessary, to produce splendid coiled pieces to your own designs.

In conclusion, coiling is a deceptively simple method of producing pots. It requires virtually no tools or equipment, is relatively clean (and certainly dry), and can be done in the simplest of work areas including, if nowhere else is available, the dining-room. If, however, you wish to rise above the 'dog bowl' and soggy pot level so often synonymous with evening class pottery you will need to be careful, and to concentrate. With perseverance you will find that the only restriction to your creative enterprises will be the size of the kiln.

7 Wheel Work

The action of making pots on some form of potter's wheel is known as *'throwing'*. Anyone who has watched a potter at work on a wheel cannot fail to have been impressed by the apparent ease with which all manner of variations on the simple cylindrical vase shape can be achieved.

Anyone trying to throw for the first time will also have been struck by the apparent waywardness of the clay, the difficulty of controlling a lump of totally inert material which seems suddenly to have taken on a life of its own. You may well be frustrated at your first attempt; some people have such negative experiences that they simply give up, considering wheel work to be beyond their capabilities.

So let us look at the factors at work to obtain a clear idea of both your own shortcomings, and what could be a lack of appreciation of other outside influences, any of which could cause problems but can be easily eliminated.

THE WHEEL

The three basic factors in the equation are a wheel, the clay, and you. In Chapter 5 on equipment and tools I examined various types of wheel, and suggested that it is probably easier to learn to throw on a powered wheel. If you have the choice you will find that a good quality electric wheel which operates smoothly, with a reserve of power rather than just excessive top speed, will allow you to concentrate on the other problems you face, rather than worrying about how to peddle the wheel and manipulate clay at the same time. Personal fit is also important – you should be able to reach the controls wherever they are situated without disruption to your working position. Where an adjustable seat is provided, try different positions to determine the best height for back comfort and foot control. If there is no seat, and you are obliged to stand on one leg you may possibly find a stool makes life easier. In any event, try to find a wheel which is comfortable and which you find easy to operate.

THE CLAY

Clay is obviously another factor which has to be given careful attention. In Chapter 2 on preparing the clay I mentioned that if you cannot knead the clay it will not be possible to throw it. It is safe to assume that most frustration experienced when attempting to throw is caused by inadequately prepared clay. It must be de-aired, both to avoid problems in the kiln later and to eliminate hard bubbles of air causing distortions when throwing. Air bubbles will feel like hard lumps in the clay as it rotates and is squeezed between your fingers. A cross-section of pot-wall might look something like the diagram over.

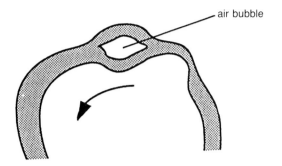

air bubble

Cross-section of a pot wall. The wall has been over-squeezed due to the involuntary action of fingers reacting against a hard lump.

The clay's consistency must be totally homogeneous, having no harder or softer areas, no air or water pockets, and no foreign bodies such as small pieces of sponge or chips of plaster. Young children sometimes pick up drawing pins and pencil sharpenings in their clay; cleaners and caretakers confuse soak-bins with rubbish bins and experienced potters misplace pieces of chamois or sponge.

Most important of all, the clay should be of a suitably soft consistency. As already mentioned, if you can knead it you can probably throw it, but it is really something each potter has to decide for him or herself based on trial and error. After a relatively short time you will get the feel for what is best for you, but to begin with avoid stiff clay. In a word – prepare.

MAKING A START

To ensure the best possible chance of success be well prepared. Having watched a tutor throw the body of a jug while explaining step by step exactly what is going on is not really enough. It can be inspiring and motivating. But it is not really preparation. In most things, learning by doing works well, and pottery is no exception. However, an understanding of what you are trying to do is necessary, and this can be obtained in some measure in advance of your first practical attempts on the wheel. Reading books can help; photographs and explanations can make sense, coupled with watching demonstrations by experts. My own view is that watching is the greatest help. If you can spare the time to watch a potter constantly in action at the wheel you will sooner or later feel a genuine urge to either copy or improve on the example set for you. An understanding of the various stages will develop, so that you feel that you can see not only what is being done and why, but possibly instances where you feel you could do a little better. You will be itching to try, impatient to have a go, and confident that in some measure you have grasped the basic stages in the process.

After watching a craftsperson at work you will have noticed several things. The clay will have been thoroughly prepared in sufficient quantity to ensure a working rhythm. Balls of clay will have been measured out and protected from the air and subsequent drying. The potter will have organised the working area so that tools are readily available; water is at hand in the wheel tray; there is something available with which to wipe off hands. Balls of clay will be stored within easy reach.

You will soon become aware of a deliberate, systematic approach to the task whereby the potter's actions are considered and methodical. You will notice that the overall process of throwing a hollow vessel has been broken down into a series of stages which may appear to flow together or may stand apart as obviously distinct steps. Whether you watch practising potters or read books it will be useful, if not imperative, to identify these stages, as each determines logically how to proceed with ease on to the next. Unfortunately, if you have been observing the attempts of an unprepared beginner, you will have noticed no such calm purposeful approach. The process will appear to be a struggle between the would-be potter and the material that person attempts to impose his or her will upon. The results can be hilarious or infuriating, but they will rarely be successful.

The overall process can be broken down into the following stages:

1 Centring the clay on the wheelhead.
2 Making a solid cone.
3 Making a solid cylinder.
4 Opening the clay.
5 Pulling up into a hollow cylinder.
6 Forming this into the desired shape.

The above is prefaced with 'preparation', without which centring will be virtually impossible. These stages can be examined individually to see how each step dictates the success or otherwise of the next.

TOOLS YOU WILL NEED

Essentials

1 Bowl of water, placed readily at hand in the wheel-tray or on a board at the rear of the tray.

2 Sponge. Small 'elephant-ear', natural.
3 A piece of ruler approximately 6in (15cm) with one end cut to dog-ear shape, of a pointed angle about 30–45 degrees.
4 Cutting wire – twisted wire or nylon, easily home-made.

Non-Essentials

5 Potter's needle – for trimming uneven rims.
6 Small sponge on a stick – for mopping out tall pots too narrow to get your hand or fingers inside. It need not be of natural sponge.
7 Potter's ribs – for shaping walls, turning down rims, smoothing bases of plates.
8 Assorted modelling tools. Used as ruler above, for marking and impressing to emphasise rims, etc.

PREPARATION

If the clay is not homogeneous and of the right consistency you will have little success.

Step 1

Centring is the process of distributing the mass of clay equally about the centre of the wheel. If clay is first made up into balls which are then placed in the middle of the wheelhead there should be fewer problems with shaping the clay. When cubes or uneven lumps of clay are plonked on eccentrically, a great deal of luck and brute force will be required to persuade the clay to redistribute evenly about the axis of the wheel.

Novices will find that it is best to place

Centring.

Step 2

Set the wheel in motion at a reasonably high speed. You will see that the wheel spins anticlockwise so that the clay is travelling towards your left side and hand, and away from you on your right. This is important to note because the next stage is to centralise the clay completely by persuading any protuberances to move inward and upward so that they appear to disappear at the top of a spiral movement. To effect this, these lumps are met by an immovable object (your left hand) as they travel round towards you (*see* below).

Lubricate the lump of clay with water. Gently squeeze a small wetted sponge out over the top of the clay. Merely dipping your hands in water will probably be insufficient; drenching the clay, on the

the ball of clay gently on to a dry wheel-head, using dry hands, directly over the centre. Holding your head directly above the wheel helps you judge the centre (*see* opposite). Use the concentric rings marked on the wheelhead to guide you, and when satisfied that the ball is central, depress it a little on to the head. Turn the wheel using your hands and firmly slap the clay as it turns, down on to the wheelhead into a cone shape so that it is stuck firmly on the dry head (*see* above). Use dry hands for this also, because if either the wheelhead or the ball of clay is wet the water or slurry will cause the clay to skid off the wheel, being unable to adhere to the watery surface. When you have hand-centred and fixed the clay you can proceed to the 'fun' part.

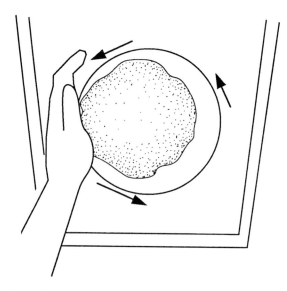

Centralising the clay. The heel of the left hand forces eccentric clay to move inward and upward.

other hand, simply causes slurry to fly everywhere. Start at the bottom of the cone, allowing the protuberances to bump into the heel of your hand rather than pushing hard yourself into the side of the clay. The lumps will be obliged to move inwards and upwards provided your hand remains firm and provided you are not 'fighting' excessive nonconformities. Remember to work in small steps, little by little, and to lubricate with water before each movement. Clay has to be coaxed gently but firmly, so be patient and you will soon be rewarded with a perfectly centred cone.

There are numerous ways of actually holding your hands against the clay. The left hand has to do the major part of the work at this stage, however, and the right hand can only support it (*see* opposite). Arms and body form a rigid triangular structure resistant to the force inflicted by mobile protuberances of clay. This structure can be reinforced by keeping elbows in to the body or placing arms firmly on to thighs or the top edge of the wheel-tray, so that wheel and body combine to form one solid structure. The intention is that you can cause the clay to move by small degrees. The clay should not be moving you. If it is, either you have not locked your hands firmly enough, or the clay is rather too firm. Another possibility is that you are trying to move too much clay in one attempt, pushing excessively with the heel of your left hand so that, after the initial pressure has moved the clay further off-centre, the momentum of the eccentric clay is just too much for your arm to resist.

Having centred a cone of clay you will have overcome the major difficulty in the whole process. It is this centring which usually causes the greatest heartache to

Coning.

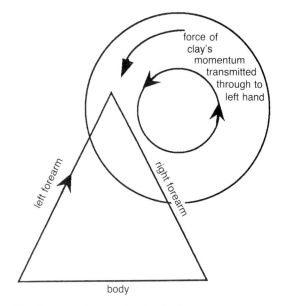

The forces acting on the clay body.

most beginners so it is well worth over-stating the probable causes of failure. Ensure that the clay is adequately prepared. Be careful to have a dry wheelhead, hands and ball of clay before attempting to stick the ball to the wheelhead. Coax the clay to move in modest steps, do not force it too far in one go. If your first attempt fails remember the above points, particularly the need for a dry wheelhead and clay ball and resist the temptation to return a soggy dollop of used clay to the wheel. Just put the used clay to one side so that it can be reprepared later, either via the soak-bin, or preferably by kneading up all your used clay at the end of the session ready to be stored for reuse, and have another attempt.

Step 3

The centred cone will now require flattening from the top to produce a solid cylinder. I use the thumb of the left hand to depress the point of the cone gently but firmly, steadying the clay with the right hand (*see* opposite). It will not be necessary to have quite such a fast wheel speed here so reduce it a little, and co-ordinate hand movement with the speed of the wheel. This should present no difficulties, and even if things do go slightly wrong all you need do is return to Step 2, coning, and restart. The solid cylinder should be thrown into a form which has a square profile.

Step 4

Like Step 1, this stage is rather critical if a successful outcome is to be achieved. I will therefore outline a few simple, obvious principles, the application of which will smooth the way towards a satisfactory outcome.

(a)   To make a hole at the centre of the clay it is essential that the clay is first centred on the wheel.
(b)   At any given motor speed the peripheral speed will be greater than the speed nearer the centre of the wheel.
(c)   A granule of clay travelling one revolution on the outside of a lump of clay will travel further than a granule nearer the centre.
(d)   Granules of clay piled up along the axis of the clay will not travel; they will simply revolve upon themselves.

To open the clay, downward pressure is applied to the centre of the top of the cylinder. As central wheel speed is virtually nil, a moderately fast speed can be applied. Keep your eyes right over the centre and pour all concentration as well as your left thumb into the centre of the revolving clay. Imagine the molecules of clay piled up along the clay's axis. You are trying to press them downwards as they rotate. Support the thumb with your right hand to maintain pressure at the exact centre and open up the clay firmly and carefully, pushing the top-most centre molecule down into the body of the clay until the end of your thumb is about a quarter of an inch (0.6cm), or finger thickness, above the wheelhead.

As you become more experienced at judging depth you will instinctively know just how far down to press without obtaining a beginner's flower pot with accidental drainage hole! A useful means of measuring inside depth against outside height is to use two pencils. One is gently laid across the top of the cylinder and the other used vertically to compare outside and inside measurements downward from the horizontal pencil or similar tool.

Initial opening.

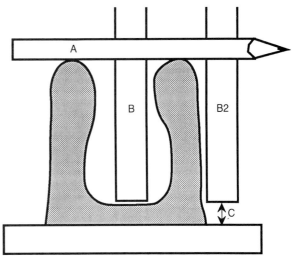

Judging depth. Hold 'B' so that the end just touches the inside bottom, with finger and thumb resting on top of 'A'. Maintain the position of grip on 'B' and move into position 'B2' so that finger and thumb again rest on 'A'. Check gap 'C' between bottom end of pencil and wheelhead. This is an excellent method for checking the thickness of the base/foot of the finished pot.

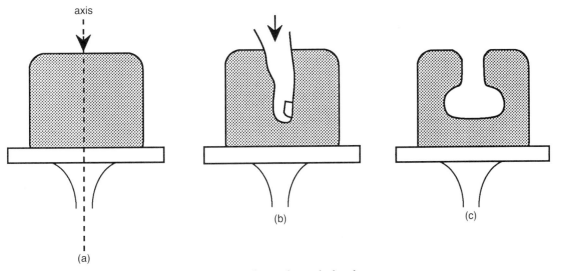

Opening the clay. (a) Imagine an axis running down through the clay.
(b) Support the thumb with your right hand to maintain pressure at the exact centre and open up the clay firmly. (c) Leave about ¼in (0.6cm) for the base.

Although actually measuring the initial opening is not essential, it can be reassuring to know that you have neither left too thick a foot already nor one so thin that when the pot is cut from the wheel there will be a hole in the bottom. In the early stages you will find it useful to check again when you have opened the clay further, as described below.

Step 5

Having opened the clay with a thumb you will now be ready to expand the opening widthwise, while preparing to stretch the clay vertically upwards. From a solid perfectly centred cylinder as in

The hands form a pincer between the left-hand fingers and right-hand knuckles.

figure (a) on page 107, you will have produced a hollow cylinder with thick, even walls.

Using your right middle finger (it's longer and stronger than the others) pinch the lower wall, applying pressure on the inside, meanwhile using your left hand to support and maintain the outside shape, as in the photograph on page 107. Leave a fat collar or flange of clay (*see* figure (c) page 107 also).

This opening up at the foot of the pot can be a critical step. Bearing in mind the principle of wheel and clay speed, any movement at and away from the centre will have to start off very slowly to compensate for the slow rotation of the clay. As the point of contact spirals outwards the clay's speed will increase so that hand movement can be speeded up in direct relation to it. Co-ordination of hand and wheel speed is always necessary, but at this particular stage a movement made too quickly from the centre outward could produce a cylinder with walls of uneven thickness.

The thick collar will be stretched or unrolled vertically upwards by a pulling action imposed from inside using the fingers of the right hand, clawing or pinching outward towards a firmly held left hand's heel and palm which are supporting and maintaining the overall width of the cylinder. As the clay stretches between the two pressure points, both hands move smoothly upwards, drawing the wall of the pot up into a more thinly walled cylinder.

It is important to use the left hand in much the same way as in Stage 1, when centring the clay. It gently but firmly maintains the outside shape, deepening the wall vertically by preventing outward expansion caused by centrifugal forces

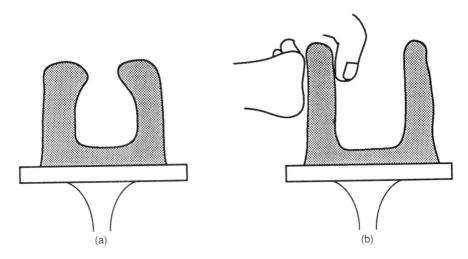

The thick collar (a) should be rolled or stretched vertically upwards. (b) This is performed by a pulling action from the inside using the fingers of the right hand.

acting on the clay. These forces become more pronounced both as wheel speed and diameter increase. Remember, peripheral speed is greater. This could be seen as a passive action as compared to the positive action of the right hand's fingers which squeeze or coax the clay upward, ultimately forming a rather thick pot, of uniform thickness, which now only requires refinement and thinning to complete the process.

Up to this point all the action has taken place on your left hand's side, with the clay travelling *towards* the points of contact. From here on, however, all the forming, shaping and refining of the form will be carried out on the right hand side, with the clay moving *away* from the points of contact.

Step 6

At this stage the walls of the clay have become relatively thin. The clay has frequently been lubricated with water, and although a vertical form will easily be supported by itself, both friction imposed by hands and finger, and further shaping can cause distortion to the form. It is therefore necessary to use minimum contact, using a knuckle or fingertip rather than the whole palm of the hand. Drawing up and shaping must be done in gentle stages. Care must be taken not to throw some parts of the walls too thin; over-lubrication can cause collapse.

Apart from the foregoing, this step is both easy and very exciting. First examine the photograph opposite, which illustrates one good way of making a pincer action using both hands. The left hand will work on the inside of the pot, tending to act outwards. The right hand, in the main the knuckle of either first or second finger, will act on the outside, opposite the left finger, producing a gentle squeezing pincer action.

As with previous steps, each movement, or squeezing action, starts at the foot of the pot and moves steadily upwards, creating the characteristic spiral markings on the vessel. Each movement,

109

Pincer in use. Note the thumb bridging the gap.

Pulling up a cylinder.

110

Forming a rim or lip.

Cleaning up the rim.

Extending height and developing shape.

A potter's rib being used to clean up the profile.

constantly lubricated to avoid friction, is continued to the top lip of the pot and beyond. Pressure is gradually released, but hands must not be snatched away; any sudden movement would cause uneven thickness of the pot wall. The upward spiralling action should, as in the foot or base of the pot, apply equal pressure to all parts of the clay. A quick action upwards, uncoordinated to wheel speed, will squeeze only a part of the whole, and alternating thin and thick spirals will give a cork-screw shape to the pot which will be difficult or impossible to correct in subsequent movements (*see* diagram opposite).

If the hollow form achieved at the end of Step 5 is reasonably thin, Stage 6 will

be easy and direct. To produce a simple but well-thrown cylinder you will only need to make one or two pinching movements, followed by a little trimming from the outside foot before cutting the finished pot from the wheelhead.

Complete throwing and clean up the pot using a squeezed out damp sponge, mopping out slurry from inside and out This cleaning-up not only enhances the visual appearance of the pot, but also removes the lubricating agent (water) which could now at best delay stiffening up, and at worst cause splitting if left on the pot. If you examine the lower outside wall you will probably find the wall of the pot slopes outward and downwards on to the wheelhead, leaving a rather

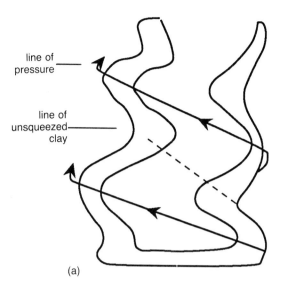

line of
pressure

line of
unsqueezed
clay

(a)

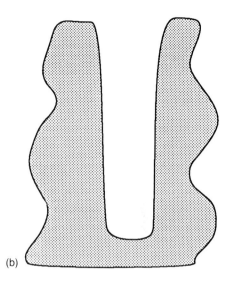

(b)

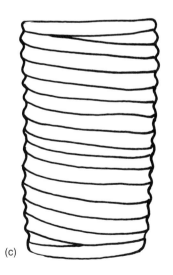

(c)

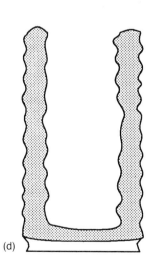

(d)

Upward spiralling. (a) The upward spiral movement was too rapid, leaving parts
of the cylinder unsqueezed, producing a violent 'open' spiral. (b) Bad spiralling,
showing uneven thickness. (c) Gently rising spiral indicates that all the clay in
the wall has been equally squeezed and stretched. (d) The cross-section of (c)
shows a general even thickness.

113

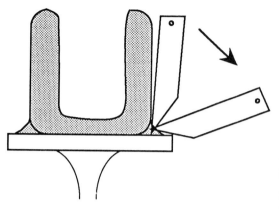

Flange of clay requires trimming to conform to the overall thickness of the pot's cross-section.

of which have their particular merits. Both are outlined below.

The pot is released from the wheel by cutting with a taut wire or nylon line. Thereafter it is removed bodily on to a suitable wooden tile or similar. The tool is easily made using fairly strong nylon fishing line, or wire about 12–14in (30–35cm) long with a button, duffle-type peg or just a piece of dowel rod attached to each end. Cutting wires which use metal rings at each end can be purchased, but these obviously do not float, and are therefore less easy to find if they fall into a wheel-tray awash with slurry and wet clay trimmings.

untidy rim-like flange. This should be cut away as indicated in the diagram above.

Cut away excess clay at the foot using a dog-ear turning tool or a home-made wooden one made out of an old 6in (15cm) ruler sawn off at somewhere between 30–45 degrees to provide a good cutting point. Hold the tool rather as you would a pen, preferably in the left hand. Work on your right-hand side, with the clay travelling away from you, and steady the tool with the right hand. As the pot revolves fairly slowly, carefully trim downwards to the wheelhead, turning the tool down to cause the trimming to twist outwards from the pot.

Step 7

The finished cylinder now has to be removed from the wheel and allowed to dry out slowly. Obviously the clay is very soft at this stage so any handling has to be done with care to avoid distortion or damage to the form. There are two variations on one method for doing this, both

A sheet of newsprint gently placed over the rim supports the elipse when the pot is removed from the wheel.

Variation A

1 Have a tile or wooden bat at the ready.
2 Wet its upper surface well.
3 Flood the wheelhead with water.
4 Keeping the wire taut and firmly down on the wheelhead, cut off the pot, allowing the wheel to turn as the wire is dragged or pushed across beneath the pot. This both releases the pot and allows a film of water to be drawn under the foot so that it can be gently slid across the wheelhead.
5 Using the outside edges of the hands, or as many fingertips as can be brought to bear, gently turn and slide the pot towards the edge of the wheel. At first it may not move, but it will soon slide easily. Apply pressure at the foot of the pot where the base can support its walls.
6 Hold the wet bat against the side of the wheel and slide the pot across on to it.
7 Mop off water from the batt with a small sponge and leave the pot safely on one side to stiffen up.

Variation B

1 Have a *dry* bat or board ready to receive the pot. *Do not wet* the wheelhead.
2 Preferably using a twisted wire cutter, cut under the foot as in 4 above.
3 Make sure your hands are clean and dry.
4 Tilt and lift the pot upwards using both hands cupped around it with most lifting being done by little fingers and outside edges of hands where the base of the pot gives support to the walls. The rest of the fingers and palms give added support, but care must be taken not to squeeze the pot out of shape. A slight twisting action coupled with the tilting

will help to release the pot which, even having been cut off the wheelhead, may be slightly reluctant to leave its birthplace.

Very smooth-bodied clays can sometimes split across the base having been wetted for removal by variation A. Some minor denting of the foot is almost inevitable, requiring turning (*see* page 119) to trim the foot finally. The main advantage of A is that everything is wet anyway and once the pot begins to move it is sometimes more convenient for cleaning up than B. Where the pot has been trimmed satisfactorily, however, B provides a clean and rather unique foot requiring no further attention other than a wipe over with a slightly damp sponge. Like most potters you will no doubt use a particular method for a particular job; you may on the other hand always prefer to use just one.

Both the above techniques work perfectly well for small pots, relatively vertical or upright pots and for smaller bowl shapes. Attempting to lift off large plates or bowls can, however, lead to tragic losses. If it is your intention to throw large pots your best course of action is to throw on bats. These are circular pieces of marine-grade plywood, or plaster of Paris, which either fix on to specially modified wheelheads or can be stuck on using clay.

College and school ceramics workshops will provide varying facilities for both wheel work generally, and for specific specialist tools and equipment such as modified wheelhead and bats. As to the merits of the systems available I will only say that I prefer simplicity. Bats held in place using clay as the adhesive have been known to slip off centre, but at

Throw a flat disc on the wheelhead.

Use a rib or similar tool to cut in grooves.

Cut across circles also.

Firmly hammer down the bat.

Centring a large ball of clay.

Remove excess water and slurry with a sponge.

Maintain a generous lip.

Develop the shape from inside.

118

Use a rib or turning tool to cut away excess clay at the foot.

Hold the tool very firmly.

least there can be no serious mechanical loss or failure; no real cost is involved, and the wheelheads revert back to normal very easily. Before purchasing a novel system for your own use it is well worth trying it out to see whether or not its advantages are outweighed by disadvantages.

Generally, irrespective of the specific system used, there is little difference between using bats and not, except that larger and broader-based pots can be removed more easily. However, when using wooden or plaster bats it is usual to dampen the upper surface of the bat before attempting to stick clay to the head. Being porous the bat has a tendency to dry out clay immediately in contact with it, absorbing moisture and reducing adhesion, this being especially true of very dry plaster. Experience will soon show you just how much dampening is required when using bats made of a particular material. It is also worth remembering that the pot requires releasing from the bat before being left to stiffen. Because it is so easy to lift bat and pot off the wheel, cutting off can sometimes be forgotten. Tension building up in the clay due to uneven drying and shrinkage could then cause splitting or warping of the pot, so do make a point of cutting through with the wire before removing from the wheel.

MORE ADVENTUROUS SHAPES

Techniques of throwing simple vertical pots on a wheel have already been described in some detail. Perhaps the next step is to attempt to form the vessel into a slightly more exotic shape. Most trad-

itional vase and jug shapes are based on an S-curve, simplified or exaggerated to produce what the potter considers to be an acceptable profile shape.

As I have mentioned previously, to draw up clay into a cylinder once it has been opened, equal pressure is applied at the same level and drawn up from the foot to the lip of the pot (*see* diagram (a) opposite).

To widen the form the inner pressure point (the fingertip, or tips, of the left hand) should be slightly higher than the outside point (the right hand). To reverse the movement, pressure points are reversed so that the outer contact is now higher. If the S-shaped profile is required the movement should again be reversed, as in (b) opposite and the following diagram.

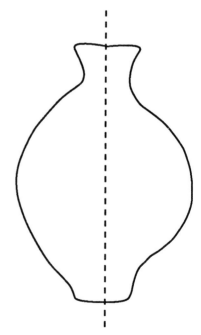

Two of the many variations possible on this simple shape. The best place to explore the range is at the wheel.

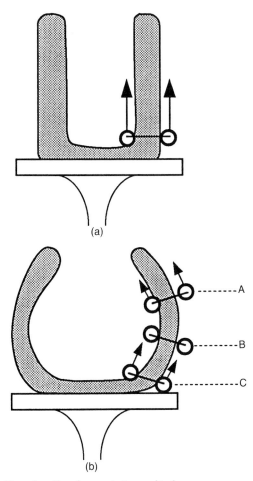

Drawing the clay up into a cylinder – use fingers or knuckles as appropriate. (a) 'Pull' is vertical and pressure points are at the same height. (b) Inside and outside contacts vary as the hands are raised towards the lip.

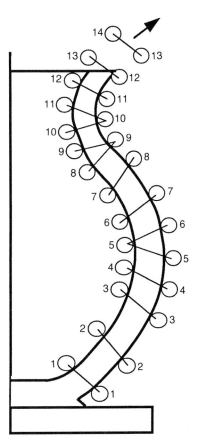

Illustrating how the main pressure is transferred from the inside hand to the outside and back again, developing an S-curve. Allow the pressure to ease at the top, but imagine that the pot is about 1in (2.5cm) higher than it is, and continue the upward movement accordingly.

Notice how the pressure point on the outside of the curve overtakes the inner one. At the innermost point on the curve the upward progress of that pressure point is slowed almost to a stop, while that on the outside of the curve speeds up. If you make a 'pinch' tool with your hands as in the photograph top left, p.123 you can adjust contact between left fingers and right knuckle, to achieve outward or inward pressure. By again using the triangular structure, with elbows in and down so that the hands are locked together at the apex of the triangle, you will have a firmly held pincer tool. The distance away from the axis of the pot can be changed slightly to follow the shape of the pot and to control its development by slightly turning your whole upper body, to move the apex inwards or outwards as necessary.

Centring.

Flattening cone. Notice the position of the hands at each stage.

Opening a solid cylinder.

Forming a hollow cylinder.

122

Pulling up.

Cleaning the form.

Developing the shape.

Working on the top.

123

Smoothing the sides.

Forming the spout.

Releasing the pot by cutting off with a twisted wire.

Use dry hands to lift pot off wheel. Note the pattern left in clay.

124

Pulling a handle.

Attaching a pre-formed slug of clay.

Gradually flatten and narrow handle appropriately.

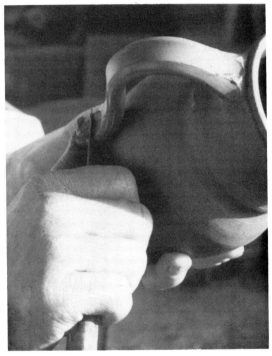

Cutting to correct length.

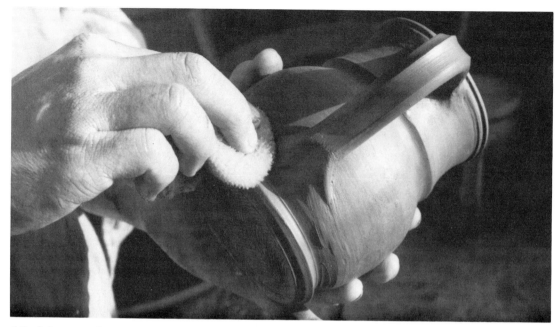

Attach lower end using sponge to clean joint.

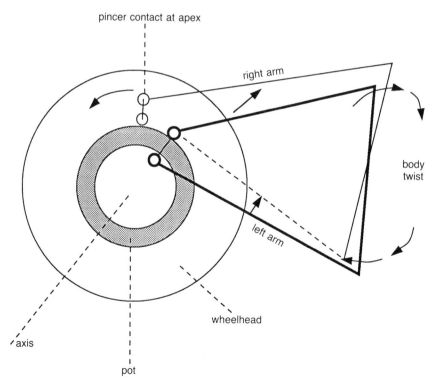

Plan view of wheel and pincer, showing twisting movement. The clay is moving away from the pincer, allowing the form to expand unimpeded. Pincer contact is moved outward as triangle twists anticlockwise.

To begin with keep the profile shape subdued, a little understated, only gradually developing the curves, a little more with each upward movement. Do not attempt to change a form from straight cylinder to an exaggerated curve in one movement as this will cause too much stress, particularly on the over-thinned and over-stretched lower regions. A wobble would then develop which could quickly become uncontrollable and the lower part of the pot would simply collapse. Experience will soon indicate the extent to which you can modify shape in one movement using a particular body prepared to your own liking.

The basic throwing technique described on page 102 can be used, with variations, for the production of most wheel-formed pieces. If, for example, outward pressure is imposed upon the cylinder in figure (a) page 128, a simple open bowl shape will develop. When a bowl is intended, however, it would be preferable to open the solid cylinder into a V-shape from the start so that form develops logically (*see* diagram over).

Work with the left hand supporting the clay as in centring. From the final V-shape the change to working on the right-hand side can be made, drawing up and out to refine the clay into the desired bowl shape (*see* photograph opposite). Try to maintain a parabolic curve on the inside of the bowl with no bump or indentation at its centre.

Most bowls have *turned* feet (*see* page 129), so either leave plenty of thickness at the foot to allow for turning, or, if the bowl is fairly small, trim off the excess flange at its foot, cut off with a twisted wire and clean up with a sponge. Soup or cereal bowls can be finished effectively without the need for turned feet.

Maintain a parabolic curve inside.

Widen, and increase height.

Bowls usually look best with a firm lip.

As you will see from the illustrations to this chapter, the basic S-curve form can be used in a variety of situations. Using small amounts of clay, narrow bottle shapes can be produced, as can spouts. A variation on the bowl can be turned and inverted to produce a simple lid.

An alternative lid can be based on a combination of bowl and plate (*see* page 130). Restrict the thickness of the base so that by cutting off with a twisted wire there will be no need to turn the lid. If this is not possible, then the lid can be turned down to an appropriate thickness and lightened in the process.

Most novices experience the problem of uneven height of walls, particularly on pots which have been narrowed at the top. This usually arises from inadequate

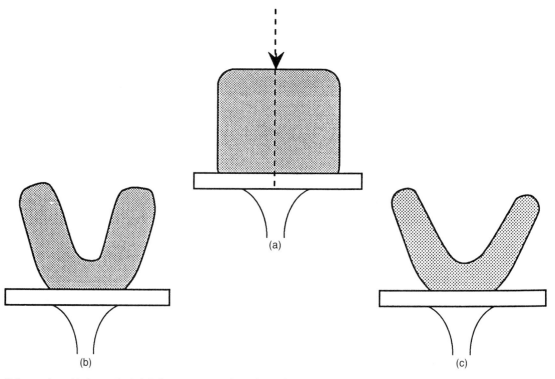

When a bowl is intended, it is best to open the solid cylinder into a V-shape.

John Pollex. 'Toft' plate, approximately 20in (51cm) diameter. Red earthenware, trail slips, 1,100°C; oxidised.

John Pollex. 'Kate's first schooldays'. Red earthenware, various coloured slips sponged and brushed, stamps and roulette to enhance decoration.

Josie Walter. 'Lobster Pot'. Oval dish 14×11in (36×28cm), decorated with two layers of paper resist, brushed, trailed and infill slips. Raw glazed, clear lead bisilicate glaze-fired to cone 03 in an electric kiln.

Martin Lewis. Coiled and pinched T
material. Slips and glazes brushed on.
1,200–1,260°C, oxidised.

Judith Wensley. Vase, thrown, 10in (25cm)
high, glazes painted and trailed. Reduced
stoneware.

Judith Wensley. Vase, thrown, 12in (30cm)
high. Barium base glaze; reduced
stoneware.

Judith Wensley. Vase, thrown, 14in (36cm)
high, coloured glazes brushed and trailed.
Reduced stoneware.

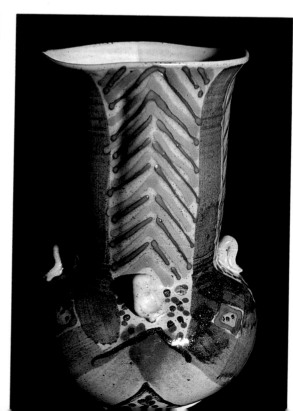

Doug Wensley. Pebble pot, coiled, approximately 22in (56cm) diameter. Slips and oxides rubbed in. Oxidised stoneware.

David Roberts. Large coil-built bottle, approximately 22in (56cm) high. Raku fired.

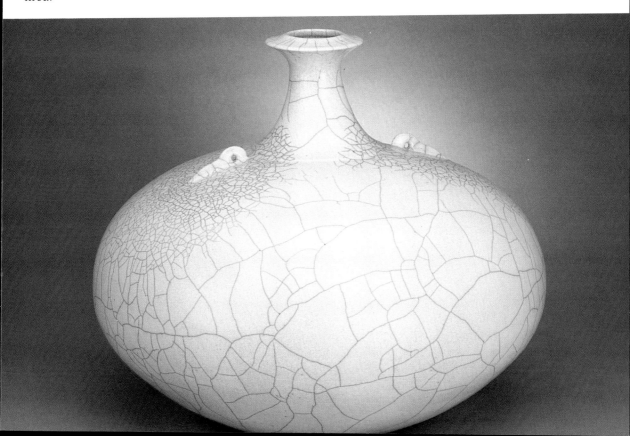

Doug Wensley. Winged pebble, coiled, approximately 22in (56cm) diameter.
Slips, glazes and body stains. Oxidised stoneware.

Doug Wensley. Pebble pot, coiled, approximately 24in (61cm) diameter. Slips
and barium glaze. Reduced stoneware.

Doug Wensley. Clefted vessel. Thrown and slabbed, approximately 15in (38cm). Stains and slips. Oxidised stoneware.

Doug Wensley. Vase construction. Slab and coil-built, 32in (81cm) high; body stains, slips and glazes. Oxidised stoneware.

Phil Jolley. Premoulded forms, 10in (25cm) high .Crank; cut and slabs added. 1,260°C; oxidised.

Judith Wensley. Bowl. Thrown, 10in (25cm) diameter. Coloured glazes trailed on to a barium base glaze. Reduced stoneware, 1,280°C.

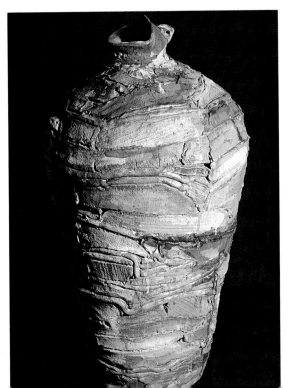

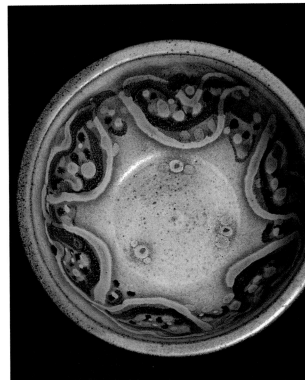

John Leach. 'Black Mood Pot'. Fired once in
a capped saggar, woodfired stoneware.

Jane Hamlyn. Teapot. Slips and impressed
decoration; saltglazed stoneware.

Doug Wensley. Sculptural form. Coiled and
slabbed, approximately 40in (102cm) high.
Saltglazed stoneware.

Doug Wensley. Sculptural form. Slabbed
and coiled, approximately 50in (127cm)
high. Slips, glazes, fibres, wood and acrylic.
Oxidised stoneware.

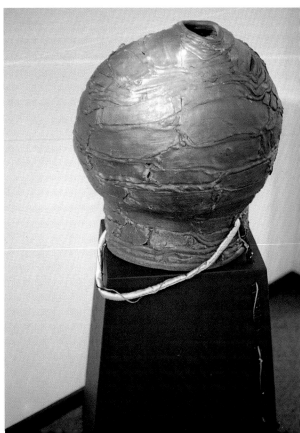

Janet Lewis. Bowl. Porcelain with lustres.
1,280°C, oxidised.

Doug Wensley. Pebble pot. Coiled,
approximately 25in (64cm) diameter. Slips
and barium glaze, oxidised stoneware.

Phil Jolley. Slab-built form, 14in (36cm) high.
Crank bodystains with inlays and slip
interior. 1,260°C; oxidised.

Doug Wensley. Vase. Thrown, two sections,
approximately 25in (64cm) high. Oxidised
stoneware.

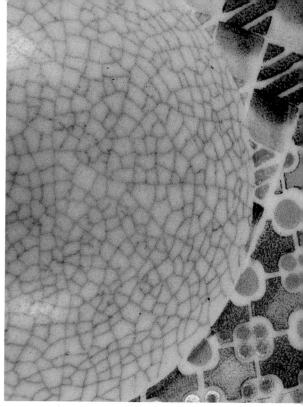

William Ruscoe. 'Shore-leave'. Direct modelling. Various coloured clays, balled, rolled, slabbed and pinched.

John Wheeldon. Detail of crackle glaze and precious lustres.

John Wheeldon. Basalt bowls (detail). Lustres on a cone 8 glaze.

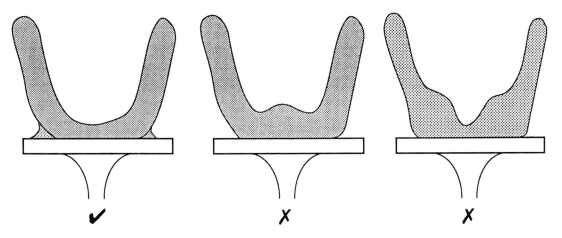

Maintain a parabolic curve on the inside of the bowl with no bump or indentation in the centre.

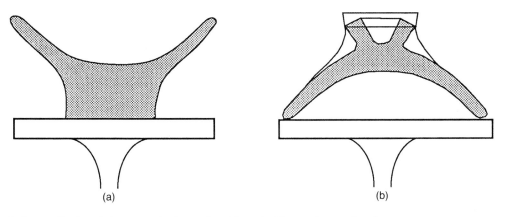

(a)   (b)

A variation on the bowl shape can be turned and inverted to produce a simple lid.

preparation, centring, or uneven opening of the clay, leaving perhaps only a very slight increase in thickness somewhere around the cylinder. This lump may have been successfully thrown upward later, only to arrive at the lip as an unwanted wave spoiling the finished line of the pot. It can, however, be easily trimmed off. Use a needle held at an appropriate height and gently pushed through the wall of the revolving pot until it is felt by a supporting finger held inside opposite the point of entry. The released rim of clay can then be lifted carefully away while the pot is still turning, leaving a clean-cut edge which now requires softening or rounding off using a damp sponge or wet fingers.

As clay-covered cork-handled needles can inadvertently become lost in clay and only reappear when stuck into fingers it may be thought worthwhile to try an alternative method, making the needle obsolete. Use a nylon cutting wire, held

129

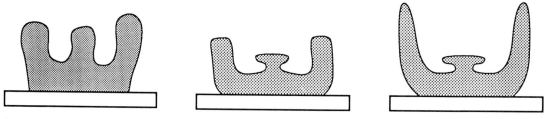

Constructing a lid based on a combination of bowl and plate.

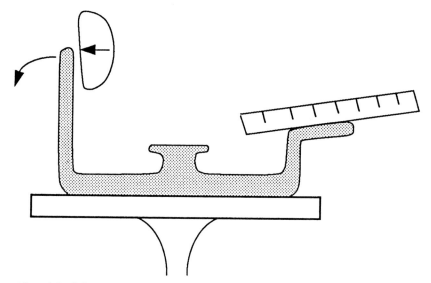

Forming the sides of the lid.

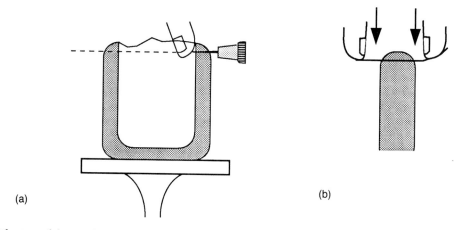

(a)

(b)

If the top of the pot is uneven, it should be trimmed. (a) A potter's needle can be used, pushed through the clay with the wheel turning. (b) Stretched nylon held between two thumbs, 1in (2.5cm) apart.

very short between two hands in such a way as to stretch the line taut between the ends of the thumbs. Using what is effectively a miniature potter's harp the offending bulge can be trimmed off by carefully cutting down from the lip as the pot revolves, levelling the cut at the appropriate height and thus trimming horizontally completely round the top of the pot.

Throwing a Plate

Apart from mugs, jugs and cups the most familiar ceramic object is probably the plate. I suspect that many a novice on her or his first evening course has secret aspirations in the general area of tea or dinner services, useful as Christmas presents, or to impress the cynical spouse. Unfortunately our familiarity is with mass-produced plates which are both very light and usually decorated with sterile glazes and screen-printed transfers. Bearing in mind, therefore, that the character of hand-thrown plates is essentially different to their factory-made cousins, and hand-making matching sets of anything is not always as precise a science as some folk would like it to be, let us look at the technique of hand-thrown plate making.

As always, clay must be centred, coned and, for plates, formed into a squat solid cylinder. The clay is opened up in much the same way as in any other situation, except that the opening can be made wider. A rib can be used (*see* diagram below) to obtain a smooth, flat base as well as to turn down the rim.

It is actually remarkably easy to produce plates in theory, but in practice there are several things which need to be born in mind. First, the plate will, regardless of size, be virtually impossible to lift from the wheel while in a plastic state. Throw the plate on a bat so that you will not be obliged to occupy the wheel for a long period of time for no good reason. When turning down the rim, avoid the absolute horizontal; the weight of the wet clay, particularly on very wide plates, will cause the rim to sag. Leave the rim sloping slightly up and outward to avoid this.

A major problem with plates is that, although it is desirable to stiffen the whole object quickly to 'fix' the shape, the rim will dry more quickly than the base. This can happen because first it has air almost all around it and second it is not resting on a damp moisture-retaining bat. The plate, therefore, has to be allowed to dry out evenly and slowly, away from draughts and sources of heat. Damp cupboards can be used, although we have

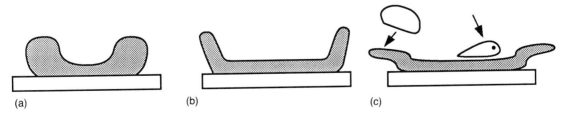

(a) (b) (c)

Throwing a plate. (a) The clay is opened up in the usual way. (b) The opening should, of course, be much wider. (c) A rib can be used to obtain a smooth, flat base as well as to turn down the rim.

found that a plastic bag from a dry-cleaner's, very thin and light, can be floated down over the plate so that it can be left somewhere safely out of harm's way. If the weather is right we sometimes give plates a quick burst of all-over fresh air and sunlight before covering, just to firm up the surfaces still wet from throwing.

A SUMMARY OF THROWING

Having read through what inevitably has to be a long and somewhat involved description of throwing techniques, you may find it helpful if the overall process is reviewed in order to clarify and focus on the most essential factors.

1   Preparation – clay, tools, equipment, including storage.
2   Centring the clay on the wheelhead.
3   Opening up the clay. For 2 and 3 work on left – clay travelling towards your left hand.
4   Shaping and refining the form – work on your right with clay travelling away from points of contact.
5   Removal and storage.

There are three main factors which determine a successful outcome:

(a)   Clay must be homogeneous.
(b)   Clay must be centred.
(c)   Clay must be opened in such a way as not to build in an exaggerated spiral and/or walls of uneven thickness.

Provided that care is taken at each stage, (a) will assist in securing success with (b). In turn, (c) depends on (b) and on wheel and hand speed. In short, the process divides up into the steps above which also fall into the two categories of working on your left and on your right. A skilled craftsperson may well appear to allow each step to flow naturally into the next, but the steps are nevertheless there to guide and aid you through the process. Perhaps the potter's motto should be, 'Preparation, Practise, Perseverance'. You may be sure that adherence to the principles contained therein will be richly rewarded.

8 Turning

When a 'finished' pot is removed from the wheel it probably has a rather thick foot which may in any case have been intentionally left that way to facilitate the turning of a ring foot or knob. It might also have become a little dented in the process of removal. In short it can require cleaning up. As suggested in the section on throwing, most if not all cleaning can be done prior to removal from the wheel, and advantage should be taken of this fact.

Ringed feet and turned knobs have to be turned later, and to do this the ware has to be firm enough to handle safely without being too dry to cut with ease. The pot should first be allowed to stiffen up to leatherhardness. This could take hours, overnight, or several days, depending on conditions at the time. The thickness of the foot must also be checked, and the wall, if it appears to need trimming; there is nothing to be gained by accidentally cutting out the bottom or through the side of the pot. So get to know it well. Use the pencil technique to sound the depth, use your eyes and hands to estimate the thickness of the lower walls. Some potters use a needle pressed through to do this. Sounds drastic, but in fact a pinprick will be of no consequence later, after the pot has been turned, fired and glazed, all of which tends to fill in or obliterate it.

Spend a little time ensuring you know where to remove clay, and how much. Having satisfied yourself that the pot is ready for turning place it upside-down centrally on a dry wheelhead. Most heads have concentric rings marked into their surfaces to guide you in this, and extra ones can be drawn on with a soft pencil if necessary. An experienced potter will place the pot more or less in place, set the wheel in motion, and neatly tap the pot smartly into the centre of the wheel. As a beginner it is best to practise this technique using bowl forms which are very stable when inverted and are less likely to be knocked off than tall shapes. A better way to practise might be to use a tin of paint, which has weight enough to prevent it from sliding too easily. It will require a fairly sharp tap but will cause no disaster if it does fall off. You could also use a small bucket of slip or glaze required for use later. Once centred on the wheel and revolving, it can be thoroughly stirred by simply holding a suitable piece of wood firmly in place as the bucket turns, saving work and effort.

Assuming a correctly centred pot, it will now be necessary to fix it in place so that pressures imposed by subsequent turning will not cause it to be moved off-centre. This is done by using three slugs of soft clay, placed at approximately 120 degree intervals around the rim of the pot. Press the clay slugs down on to the head so that they stick to it and to the bowl. As this clay is much softer than the pot being held in place, it will not adhere permanently and will peel

Fixing the pot to the wheel.

away easily when turning is completed. Take care to hold the pot in place with one hand so that it is not inadvertently pushed off-centre while applying the affixing slugs.

The process of cutting away unwanted thickness from walls and hollowing out footrings requires a few rather specialist tools. These are discussed elsewhere, but they fall broadly into two categories – hooped tools which cut and allow the turnings to curl through the hoop away from the cutting area, and turning tools which scrape clay from the surface of the pot, having cutting corners and edges. Old paint scrapers make excellent turning tools. These tools should be kept sharp. It is surprising just how abrasive leatherhard clay can be, particularly

where a body contains particles of grog. It is useful, therefore, to have a grindstone or file at hand; giving the edge a little 'tooth' can make the tool a little more effective. It is also important that cutting edges cannot move independently when in use. They must be firmly fixed to handles and tightly held to prevent juddering and chattering, and to ensure that only the required depth of cut is made.

Turning a leatherhard pot is quite similar to turning wood on a lathe. The major difference is that pots are turned on a vertical axis, using the wheelhead as a chuck, rather than horizontally. The idea is to cut away unwanted material by allowing the pot to spin or turn on the wheel so that non-conforming bumps are

Using a turning tool.

brought into contact with an immovable object, in this case a sharp tool, acting in a similar manner to that of the left hand when centring. In practice, of course, the tool does move as it is brought carefully into position, gradually cutting away protuberances and producing first a uniform flat foot, and then a clean, circular outer edge of rather larger diameter than required for the final foot. The foot may well be found to be level before turning, provided that care was taken to keep the wire taut and hard down on the wheelhead when the pot was cut off the wheel. If so you will have been spared some work.

This solid foot can then be hollowed out, producing a more elegant conclu-sion to the pot, lighter and less prone to firing difficulties. Start in the centre, probably using a hooped tool, working outwards, and cutting into the foot in shallow furrows. Too deep a cut could cause the pot to be snatched off the wheelhead, acting too much as a brake on the revolving pot. So do not be tempted to take off too much clay in one cut; it is safer to take your time. Cut outwards to within about 1in (2.5cm) of the edge, leaving a rim rather wider than will ultimately be required. When a satisfactory depth is reached inside the foot the rim can be turned down inside and out as necessary to create a neat foot of appropriate proportion to the overall form of the pot.

Turning out the centre of a foot ring.

Finishing the foot ring.

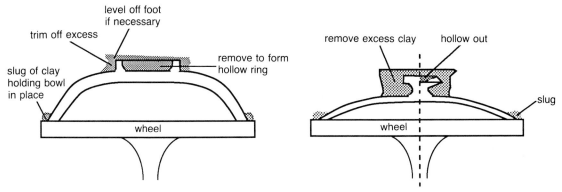

Hollowing out a solid foot or lid handle produces a more attractive pot.

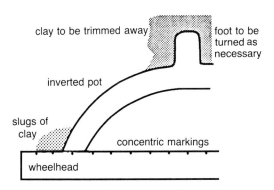

The foot is turned to smooth off any sharpness.

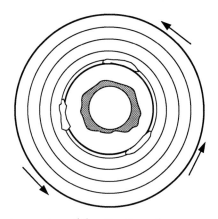

Potter's eye view of the situation when turning a foot or handle.

To add the final touch to the turned pot, a smooth flat tool such as a wooden modelling tool, an old spoon or a thumbnail can be used to burnish, or smooth, the turned surfaces. This may not be considered absolutely essential, but it does ensure that grog contained within the clay body is pressed down particularly on the foot, where contact could be made with furniture or other surfaces prone to scratching. It also enhances the visual appearance of the pot at this stage, and shows that you care about it.

A lid can be made using the same technique as above, throwing the bowl shallow enough to suit the container for which it is intended. Measure width using callipers as shown elsewhere to ensure correct fit. Remember to leave the base thick enough to allow a knob to be turned out of it.

With practice both centring and turning will become almost second nature to you, and you will certainly be surprised at the limitless range of possibilities available, and pleased by the degree by which your pots are 'professionalised' by suitable turning.

9 Firing

AIMS

When an object has been made in clay there are a number of things yet to be done before it can be considered ceramic. Clay has to be plastic for it to be possible to model and mould it into the required form. In truth, the material is wet. Its condition is both temporary and vulnerable. Once dried out, the clay becomes rigid and fixed, but is still fragile. And it still contains chemically bound-up water in its structure. When this water is driven off by the application of heat, the clay undergoes a one-way process of change, becoming harder. When sufficient heat-work has been achieved the material also becomes more durable. The pattern of metamorphosis is as follows:

1   At room temperature the clay loses free moisture and slowly dries, often taking several days, or even weeks. Initial shrinkage takes place.
2   When subjected to a temperature of about 100° centigrade any remaining free water will be driven off. This can be achieved in a kiln or other heating appliance.
3   Water chemically bound up in the clay's molecular structure will be driven off when the temperature is increased beyond 600° centigrade. The body will be very fragile at this stage, being soft and of no practical use. Further shrinkage

takes place as a consequence of this loss.
4   Beyond 850–900° centigrade the body is hardened sufficiently to be considered more or less durable, although it is porous.
5   At about 1,100° centigrade it has become hard enough for use as a container and to be picked up under load. It is of course susceptible to breakage from impact shock. The body remains porous.
6   Beyond 1,150° centigrade most clay bodies begin a second metamorphosis whereby they fuse so as to become non-porous, or vitrified.
7   If the temperature is allowed to rise beyond vitrification point, a body will literally begin to melt.

The initial purpose of firing a clay object, therefore, is to transform the clay into a new and stronger material. To do so it is necessary to apply heat very gradually, particularly in the early stages, and to control the ultimate temperature achieved.

The novice will sometimes enquire as to the possibility of using a domestic oven to render clay hard. The short answer is that it is not suitable. Most cookers have an approximate maximum temperature of about 475° fahrenheit. The temperatures required for ceramic purposes are often in excess of five times that, so no useful purpose is served by attempting such a procedure.

BISCUIT WARE

When the hardening process has been carried out and the raw clay changed into a relatively hard porous state it can be handled with comparative safety and will withstand absorption of moisture without disintegrating. This new material is usually referred to as biscuit ware, partly because of its ability to absorb moisture and partly because many buff and grey clays burn to a light toasted biscuit colour. When red clays are so fired they become the traditional terracotta colour familiar as the flowerpots and chimney pots of bygone years. But as vessels they lack some of the necessary qualities. Such porous bodies would be unacceptable for use as cups or mugs because of their objectionable feel to the lips and their tendency to become rancid when in use. Their use as liquid storage containers would be very restricted, for similar reasons.

EARTHENWARE

Biscuit ware and some glazed ware are produced within the same temperature range. Porous bodies, glazed over, are known as earthenware. Arguably the only difference between them is that the latter has a glazed surface. Porous biscuit ware is given a coating which, under the influence of a further firing, will form a glassy covering over the body, protecting and enhancing its appearance at the same time. When fired beyond about 1,150° centigrade red terracotta clays begin to vitrify. Buff clays will require temperatures approaching 1,250° centigrade before they change.

This metamorphosis, brought about by temperatures which vary depending on the type of clay being fired, is very significant to potters, indicating as it does the advent of another new material.

STONEWARE AND PORCELAIN

When fired to high temperatures in the region of 1,250–1,280° centigrade grey clays vitrify and are subsequently referred to as stoneware. The essential difference here is that the body becomes impervious to moisture, can therefore be used for domestic and sanitary wares, and does not actually need glazing in order to fulfil its function. Glazes applied to high-fired stoneware and porcelain are purely cosmetic.

Bodies used for stoneware are usually grey, and contain refractory material in the form of grog. This granular material, being already shrunken by its contact with heat, will be unaffected by further firing and will act as a support for the clay as it approaches its point of collapse. Some bodies contain very fine particles of refractory material, others are stiffened up with quite coarse grog which can be rather abrasive to the hands when throwing. When vitrified, the body will be non-porous but opaque, even if very thin.

Porcelain bodies are normally blended to provide an extremely fine, white body which reaches a critical point of partial collapse and fires to a vitreous but translucent white. Some light will actually pass through thinner parts of a porcelain piece, giving it an exquisitely delicate quality unique to the material. Some porcelain bodies are easier to throw than others, but most are less plastic than stoneware, and can be rather difficult to

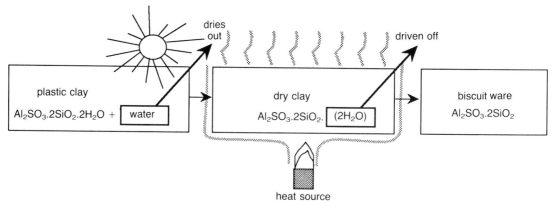

clay ($Al_2SO_3.2SiO_2.2H_2O$) = alumina + silica + water driven off by fire

The chemical changes clay undergoes during drying out and firing.

fire if made up into delicate sculptural forms. They often require external support in the fire. Features at risk can be supported by carefully inserting props made of the same body, which will fire with the piece and be removed after.

The changes which take place during drying out and subsequent firings are an integral part of the ceramic process. Plastic clay is actually clay with added free water. Dry clay also contains water. During the sequence of ceramic events all of this water is removed.

In Chapter 9 we will develop the idea of glazes a little further, when discussing the means of applying them. The idea of compiling your own glaze recipes will be discussed a little further also when discussing glaze preparation and application.

PACKING A KILN

Techniques for packing kilns vary only in as much as although raw, unglazed wares can be placed in contact with each other, glazed wares must not. In both cases a good solid pack, making max-

imum use of setting space, should be aimed at. Not only does this make good economic sense but it also assists even firing and a good atmosphere in the chamber.

Packing Biscuit Ware

Raw pots must always be handled with care and this is particularly true when packing them. The main preoccupation is often to try to find something to fit a particular space rather than to take note of exactly where a handle might be relative to the kiln wall. Care must be taken to avoid even very slight accidental contact which will inevitably result in damage. When lifting unfired wares, ensure that they are supported from beneath, putting a hand under the foot and steadying the pot with the other. Do not pick up raw pots by handles or spouts.

With care, small pots can be placed inside larger pots, and similar-sized pots can be stacked one on top of the other. One bowl can be inverted on another and the pattern repeated several times, possibly to the top of the chamber. Obviously, vessels with vertical walls provide better support than very shallow, open

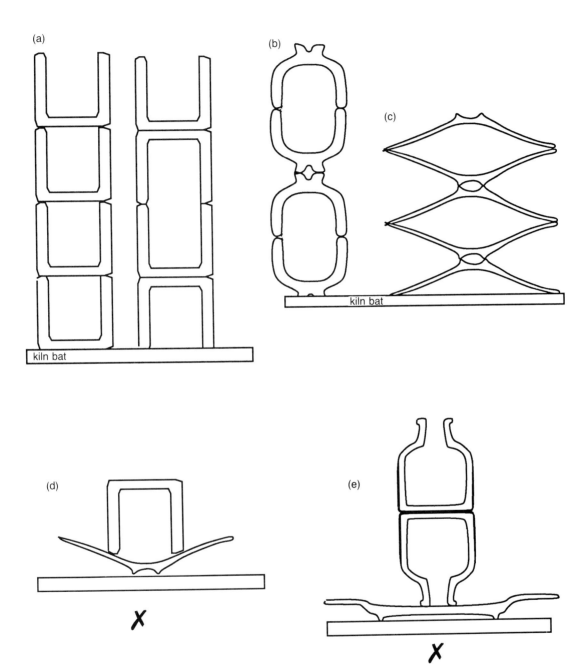

Packing biscuit ware. (a) Allows maximum support. Vertical walls carry the
weight straight down on to the kiln shelf. (b) Shapes with a concave interior
provide good support, utilising the circular structure to carry the load. (c)
Greater stress is imposed on 'coathanger' curves, particularly when the pieces
are extremely shallow. Do not over-stack such shapes. (d) and (e) show two
unsuitable methods of stacking.

141

forms. Care should be taken not to impose too much stress on such walls which would almost certainly be split under the strain. This can be a problem if packing school work, for example, when few sizes conform and shapes are less than uniform. If in any doubt, put in a shelf rather than put work at risk. When stacking odd shapes try to find solid and heavy forms for the bottom, keeping shallow, open forms to be placed at the top. Remember that pots under stress during firing are more at risk than when simply stacked in a cool kiln. So although everything might look all right survival at this point does not guarantee eventual success. Provided wares are placed in the setting chamber with due regard for weight, and are stable enough not to shift in firing, there should be no problems.

Packing Glazed Wares

Packing a glaze kiln requires that pots should not be in contact. As a general rule, if you can get a finger between items they will fire without problem. If the gap is less, glaze can pull across, joining up between two objects. And of course if there is glaze on the foot of a pot it will melt and fuse the pot to the shelf, or bat as it is properly known. Again as a general guide all glaze material should be removed, or prevented from getting there in the first place, from the foot and for about ¼in (0.6cm) up the pot's wall (*see* page 181). This will allow a slight downward movement of fusing glaze if it becomes too viscous. This technique is suitable for all temperature ranges, is probably the most reliable, and is certainly the cheapest. If bats are given a coating of bat-wash also, there should be little risk of adhesion.

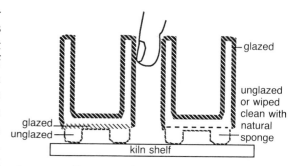

Leave a sufficient gap between glazed wares in the kiln to prevent glazes pulling across from one ware to the next.

When glazing earthenware bodies it is sometimes felt necessary to glaze the whole item to make it absorption-proof. In such cases wares are supported on stilts or spurs, refractory pieces providing support with minimum contact to glazed undersides of wares. By elevating the glazed surface above the surface of the bat and having minimum contact with the pot via only three sharp points which are chipped off after firing, virtually no part of the pot's surface remains unglazed. When pots are removed from the kiln stilts can be released from bases by easing or tapping with a sorting tool or screwdriver and used at least a few times if they are not too damaged by the glaze and removal process. Small particles of very sharp refractory material may remain stuck to the glaze. These should be carefully removed using a sorting tool and then rubbed down with a piece of carborundum stone or similar to clean up the foot. Take care not to run a hand over the foot of a pot before ensuring that every slither of refractory has been removed, because whenever there is broken ceramic material there will be razor-sharp edges. When chipping off it is advisable to wear protective goggles too.

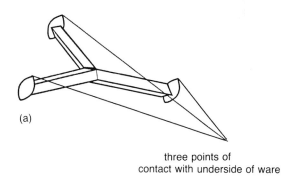

(a)

three points of
contact with underside of ware

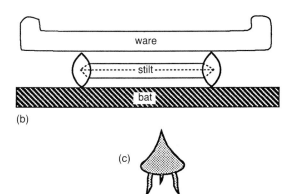

(b)

(c)

When glazing the whole of a piece, use stilts
or spurs to ensure minimum contact
between the base and the kiln shelf. (a)
Stilts. (b) Cross-section of the stilt in use. (c)
Spurs are an alternative to stilts; used in
threes, they can be arranged to suit any size.

It is inadvisable to use stilts or spurs to
support stoneware due to the tendency
of the body to warp. At peak temperature the body is approaching the point of
collapse and will sag around a stilt with
the very real possibility of falling sideways, not only collapsing itself but also
damaging other pieces in the process.
Wares with glazes in a state of flux com-
ing in contact with each other and kiln
walls can create a dreadful amount of
damage when, as the firing cools, glazes
weld everything together.

When firing very small glazed pieces
such as ceramic jewellery, nichrome wire

can be used as a support. Beads or ear-
rings which are glazed all over and
strung up between two supporting props
can be safely fired in this way. Small
items can often be packed into spaces too
small or the wrong shape to fit larger
items, and an even more economical setting can be achieved.

Kiln Furniture

Kiln furniture is necessary to support
wares in the kiln. Shelves, props and
other accessories are usually made from
high-grade alumina refractories so that
they will withstand working temperatures up to 1,300° centigrade. Furniture
as supplied with a kiln may not be to
excess in terms of quantity but should be
of appropriate dimensions to carry any
conceivable loads packed into that kiln.
The trick is to have shelves, or refractory
bats as they are known properly, of sufficient thickness to carry the weight likely
to be applied over their span. Bats of
excess thickness will absorb heat (and
money), which could be better used for
firing wares.

Bats, or kiln shelves, are rather expensive items so are worth looking after carefully. Before use ensure that bats are dry,
and not cracked. Check for cracks by
supporting the suspect bat at its centre
by hand or suspending it between thumb
and finger. Tap the bat with a metal tool.
If it rings clearly it should be sound. If
the sound is muted there is likely to be a
crack. If wet the ring will be dull. Bats
should always be stored on edge in a dry
place.

To prevent bats absorbing glaze or
being contaminated by direct contact
with it they should be coated with a
proprietory bat wash. A 50/50 mixture of

zircon and china clay will probably do just as well. Do not coat props or kiln bricks.

Props and large pots create 'hot spots' on a cooling bat. Do not 'crack' or open the kiln prematurely or uneven cooling will result, possibly damaging wares and causing glazes to craze.

Do not place bats right up against kiln walls and ensure that air can circulate throughout, possibly by leaving gaps between bats, particularly in large kilns where they are used in pairs or quadruplet.

If overall bat dimensions are kept to a minimum, their thickness and conse-quent bulk or volume can also be reduced. Where two half-sized bats are used instead of one of full size they can be correspondingly thinner. Where four 'quarter' shelves are used it is not possible to use a three-crop system so rather more setting area is encroached upon.

In the diagrams of shelf arrangements below it can be seen that, assuming that in each case the overall size is the same, plan (b) is the least impinged upon by props, although (a) might actually be better if setting one large plate on each level. Plan (c) might be more useful for this purpose than (d). In the case of (e) there

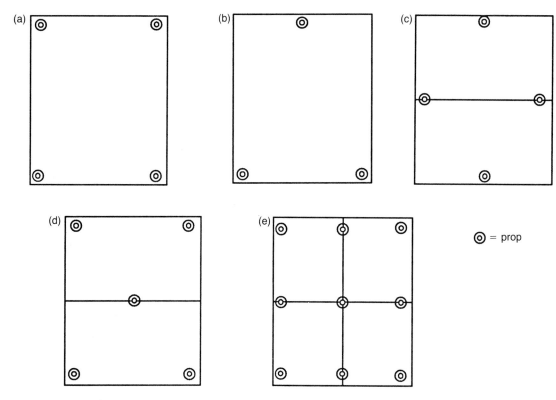

Arrangement of shelves and props within a kiln. (a), (b) and (c) All three may collapse under a very heavy load placed in the unsupported centre. Otherwise, they are well supported. (d) Slightly restricted placing, but shelves are well supported. (e) This gives maximum support for high firings and has the advantage of easier handling of the smaller bats when placing and unpacking.

might be considerable loss of setting space depending on size of pots. In any event kilnsetting can be something of a puzzle, and it is often necessary when packing assorted shapes and sizes to unpack and start all over again.

When building up layers of shelves, prop systems should be vertically in line wherever possible, especially at the bottom of the pack. Where a bat is supported at the outer edges but loaded to excess centrally there is liable to be considerable stress on it. At the higher temperatures required to fire stoneware in particular, bats can and do bend or even split. Bats and props carrying the weight of upper layers must be well supported above and beneath so that weight is transferred vertically down to the kiln floor without causing undue stress. Only in the very top layer or two may props be moved over to accommodate oddshaped pieces, and only then when it is clear that props and bats will not be transferring weight to a critically weak part of the structure. In order to spread load more evenly props can be fitted with collars, top and bottom, as shown in the diagram below.

Thermocouples can sometimes be accidentally damaged when placing pots. The porcelain sheathing is obviously fra-

(a)

(b)

Arrangement of prop systems. (a) The weight of shelves plus load is carried down by the props placed vertically in line. This arrangement should be very stable. (b) The second shelf from the bottom would be liable to central stress, and the third shelf could be warped by the lack of support at its outer edges. The fourth shelf up is liable to stress centrally, not so critically as the second (which also carries the weight of the upper layers).

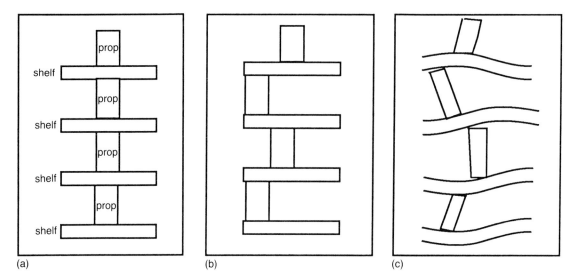

(a)   (b)   (c)

The correct and incorrect way to arrange props. Arrangement (b) would probably result in disaster (c) during firing.

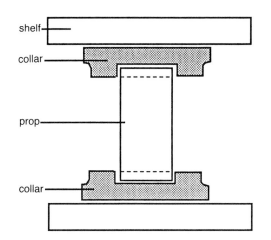

Prop collars, used to spread load more evenly.

gile, so take care not to knock it. The instrument can gently be partly withdrawn so that it does not protrude into the setting space while pots are being placed. Do not forget to replace the thermocouple before firing, and before doing so check that nothing is in its way before easing it into place.

There is a special satisfaction in achieving a good pack. Whether biscuit or glaze, it is good to know that you have made maximum use of available space and have ensured a safe firing also by your careful placing of the wares. The stage which follows is at least as satisfying, but is also an exciting challenge. A very first firing can also be a somewhat daunting experience and nerve-racking to say the least. But if the principles are reasonably well understood before the first switch is thrown the whole process is likely to be trouble free.

FIRING A KILN

If you have recently set up your own workshop or a pottery workshop in a school your first firing should logically be for biscuit. All wares to be fired must be thoroughly dry. If there are excessively thick or heavy pieces among the work these might be best left until the next firing, stored on or above the kiln so that they can benefit from the kiln's heat. The purpose of a biscuit firing, as has been said, is to drive off the water chemically combined in the clay, and to convert the material into a new form strong enough to support itself when handled. Biscuitware is therefore much easier to glaze than raw ware.

The dry, raw clay requires very slow, gentle heating in the early stages. Heat has to penetrate through the body gradually enough to prevent expansion of the surface clay while material within remains cool. If the surface expanded, this would result in surface clay breaking off in much the same way as rock breaks up if exposed to constant changes of extreme temperature. At the same time, chemically combined water has to be given the chance to escape without damaging the wares due to excessive build-up of pressure within the body.

Let us, then, look at a possible procedure for firing a small electric kiln. This could be an older model used in a home workshop and not fitted with an electro-mechanical interlock to isolate the mains supply before the kiln can be opened. Such an arrangement would not nowadays be considered acceptable in terms of safety, but used with care in a situation safe from casual and curious interference from innocents of all ages, it need cause no threat to life and limb.

Before closing the door, check the pyrometer reading. The instrument will be calibrated in degrees centigrade, so should be reading about room temperature, or 15–22° centigrade, depending on conditions at the time. If it has a digital readout it will be accurate and easy to read. If it is of the traditional analogue type it will be more difficult to obtain a precise reading, but a rough idea can be obtained as to whether or not it is wildly inaccurate and in need of recalibration. If the reading appears to be a little above or below the expected room temperature reading, more accurate readings can later be calculated by adding or subtracting the estimated discrepancy. Use cones to ascertain precise heatwork done.

If the kiln is fitted with a removable bung in the top of the chamber, remove this and close the door. Water vapour can escape easily as it is released. Where no such bung exists, it may be necessary to leave the door or lid slightly ajar. Where there might be any possibility of someone inadvertently opening the kiln while current is switched on the door must be locked in position in some way. A padlock and chain may suffice. Water vapour will require the merest crack in order to exit the chamber, so it will be impossible for anything else to be introduced into the kiln.

The kiln can now be switched on. Using Sunvic or other control switches set at low, or about 10–20 on the dial. The elements should be activated to warm the kiln slowly. Traditionally an overnight low temperature soak is used to build up gradually to 100° centigrade or a little more, allowing moisture gradually to disappear. By morning it will be possible to increase the power slowly to bring the temperature up to about 500–600° centigrade. Adjustment of the sunvic setting and careful checking on time and temperature increase should all be noted in a firing log in order to get to know the mannerisms of your equipment. With a little experience it may be possible to increase the rate so that the overnight soak builds to 200–300° centigrade.

After the soak, close the door or lid completely and continue firing. Keep any spy-holes open and/or bungs out until 600° centigrade has been reached, then close them up. Beyond this temperature it will be safe to increase power to maximum, allowing the temperature to rise at the best rate possible for the kiln until the required temperature is reached (check the cones and the pyrometer). All bungs and spyholes will be shut.

Switch off the power and allow the kiln to cool down in its own time. Do not be tempted to 'crack' the door or lid until the temperature is down to 100° centigrade. Bungs and spyholes can be opened a little earlier if required, but care should be taken not to allow a major inrush of cold air which would obviously cause great trauma to the wares, either at the above suggested temperature or higher. Gloves can be used for unpacking hot wares, but wherever possible leave everything to cool sufficiently for removal using bare hands. If the kiln is again left overnight the temptation to stay in bed will hopefully exceed the temptation to open the kiln before it has cooled sufficiently!

If a firing log is kept you will not only have a record of pots and firings but also a clear indication of temperature build-up on each occasion. It will be very useful to compare, for instance, overnight soaks started at varying times to what temperatures are achieved by morning using the same sunvic settings. You will build up a picture of the capabilities of your kiln in terms of hourly temperature increase. Expertise and confidence will grow with your ability to manage firings effectively and without undue apprehension. After all, people have been doing such things with much less

sophisticated facilities for thousands of years, so with only a few simple cones to indicate progress in an electric kiln, you can too.

Glaze Firing

One well-packed biscuit kiln will provide enough wares for at least two or three glaze firings, so you will get rather more practice of this type of firing. The main difference is that, at least in theory, the kiln can be switched to full power from the start. Due to the fact that when pots are glazed they tend to absorb free moisture, it would seem sensible to ensure a gentle drying before subjecting them to too much thermal shock. Even where the pots can withstand such shock, the glazes may not. There would be almost nothing worse, when opening a glaze kiln, than to find glaze lifting off the surfaces of wares, flaking off and pooling on the bats, causing chaos and waste. Completely dried glazed wares should never produce such an effect, but where pieces are not handled in strict rotation damp ones will inevitably be picked up. Provided that the initial temperature rise to 100° centigrade is gradual, there should be no cause for worry. Once the kiln is packed and ready for firing up there is nothing to be lost by starting as for a biscuit firing, except that there is no need for an overnight soak. Just let the temperature build up to 100° centigrade or so over a couple of hours and then apply full power.

When firing up our hypothetical elderly electric kiln we will almost certainly find that the rate of temperature increase is reasonably quick in the early stages, but falls off dramatically at the top end. It may take an hour or more to realise the final half-century of heat and as a consequence the heatwork done will be rather more than would be the case where temperatures continued to rise very rapidly. The glaze, therefore, will have had sufficient time at the point of fluxing to have matured adequately without the need for a prolonged exposure to the maximum temperature. Most glazes improve with a little 'soak', however, and with more recently developed hi-tech kilns there may well be a definite need to hold the temperature for a specific period of time depending on the glaze. This will be recommended by the supplier if you are using a commercially prepared glaze. If it is one you are developing yourself it may be a case of trial and error over several firings before the best results are achieved.

As wares contained in our firing have now a coating of essentially glassy material which, like glass, is susceptible to temperature change, it is necessary to again protect them from cold draughts and thermal shock. Slow cooling is necessary, particularly at the end of the cycle when it is all too tempting to open a kiln door to see the results of your labours. Cold air causes glaze on the surface of the pot to contract rapidly with consequent crazing of its surface. Glazed wares should therefore be left *in situ* until hand-cool before removal, particularly in the case of earthenware which obviously loses part of its usefulness once its surface is broken.

The ultimate objective when firing any kiln is to bring wares safely up to the appropriate temperature and down again. Time spent in the kiln by these pieces is not in itself any sort of measure of the work done. But often time does to some extent determine the way in which the objective is achieved, or not, as the case might be. In a school, for instance, it may not be possible to carry out overnight firing. It may, on the other hand, be possible for a pre-set kiln to be switched on very early in the morning. The person responsible can then take over during the day, leaving a kiln-sitter or some other form of control unit to complete the schedule during the evening. Ideally a kiln used in such a situation should be fitted with one of the programmers that provide fully automatic control over a complete firing sequence.

FIRING A GAS KILN

A problem with some gas-fired kilns which are built with modern materials is that they are inclined to fire too rapidly. When firing commences, therefore, care is needed to adjust burners to burn low enough without risk of flame failure. Another problem encountered later on in the schedule is that of atmosphere. When a kiln approaches maximum temperature there is likely to be a slight overstoking so that some fuel does not burn clearly. A smoky atmosphere results, which has an interesting effect on wares. This is discussed on page 187. The problem consequent on this occurrence is that it may be virtually impossible to see the cones.

Care should be taken to ensure good sight under normal conditions. Placed too near the spyhole it may be difficult to decide which cone is which, particularly if one has gone down without your noticing. I always arrange them from left to right so that they fall to the left. I use a candle or torch inside the kiln when setting to check on visibility and I try not to place them too near or too far away. They are best viewed against a plain background, either seen against one large pot or with nothing immediately behind. When other vague outlines can also be seen it is often difficult to decide what is and what is not a cone. A dark blue glass filter can be used to view through, and it sometimes helps to leave the spyhole open a moment or two to allow the atmosphere immediately inside to clear. But the best method is constant vigilance. If possible use a pyrometer as a general guide to progress. It will warn you of the approaching critical period before it happens so that you will be able to identify all three cones before the first goes down.

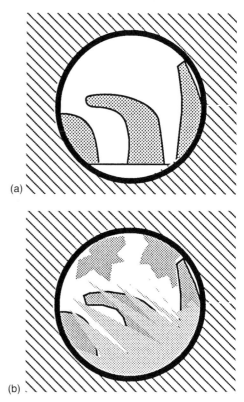

(a)

(b)

View through the spyhole. (a) At best it is often difficult to arrange cones for easy viewing. (b) If the background is confusing and the atmosphere smoky it will be more difficult to read the cones.

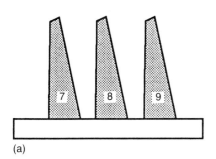

(a)

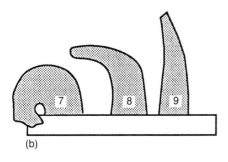

(b)

Arrangement of cones. (a) Incline cones slightly at angles to avoid them bending forward or backward. (b) Cone 7 (control) is down, cone 8 is at the quarter hour. Cone 9 is beginning to be affected. For stoneware fired to 1,250° centigrade, this would be the time to shut down the fire.

Gas kilns and their burners and controls differ from model to model. It would not be appropriate, therefore, to give a blow-by-blow description of how to fire a particular kiln. A few suggestions might be in order, nonetheless.

Igniting a gas kiln can be rather a tricky operation if you have to rely on matches. A gas poker will make it that much easier. Familiarise yourself fully with operating instructions accompanying burners and particularly flame-fail devices. It can be very frustrating to discover that for some reason the machinery has conspired against you to prevent ignition. Usually this happens if something has been done out of sequence, so read the blurb. Once lit and with burners turned up to full power, the sequence becomes similar to that of an electric kiln. While temperature builds all you can do is wait. It pays to watch and listen so that if for any reason the firing is automatically shut down you will notice and set it off again. You will also be at hand to notice that either the pressure gauge is showing a need for a new cylinder or a less intense sound will suggest the same thing. In this respect it is useful but not essential to fit a two-way valve system, enabling you to switch from one gas bottle to another without disconnection and subsequent loss of flame.

Bending temperature of cones at a temperature rise of 150° centigrade per hour:

Temperature Degrees centigrade	Harrison Cone	Orton Cone	Comments	Kiln Interior
100	–	–	boiling point – free water driven off — crack kiln door	
200	–	–	bungs out	
300	–	–	in excess of domestic cookers — biscuit slowly up to here	
400	–	–	chemically compounded water driven off	red glow appears and steadily increases
500	–	–	bungs in	
600	–	–		
700	–	–	bodies harden — rate of firing increased	
720	018			
747		017	lead glazes (Galena) (700–800)	
770	017			
792		016		
795	016			
804		015	lustres fire on	
805	015			
830	014			
838		014		
852		013	between 850° and 900°	
860	013		slow firing for	
884		012	approximately	
885	012		enamels fire on — ½–1 hour	
894		011		
910	010		carbon soak as necessary	
923		09		
930	09			
950	08			
955		08		
984		07		
990	07			

Temperature Degrees centigrade	Harrison Cone	Orton Cone	Comments	Kiln Interior
999		06		red heat –
1,015	06			bright cherry
1,040	05		soft, biscuit	
1,046		05	(porous)	
1,060	04	04	earthenware and	
1,070	04A		bone china glazes	
1,080	04B			
1,090	04C			
1,100	04D		hard earthenware glazes	bright orange red
1,101		03	usually 1,100°c maturation,	
1,115	03		some with short soak	
1,120		02	(30 min)	
1,125	02		red bodies begin to lose porosity	
1,137		01		
1,145	01		red clay vitrifies dark brown	
1,154		1	overfired begins to blister	
1,160	1			brilliant orange
1,162		2		
1,165	2			
1,168		3		
1,170	3			
1,185		4		
1,190	4			
1,196		5		
1,205	5			orange turning yellow to white
1,222		6		
1,230	6			
1,240		7		
1,250	7		grey clays begin to vitrify	
1,260	8			
1,263		8	stoneware glazes mature,	
1,280		9	also soft porcelain	
1,285	9			white
1,305	10	10	hard porcelain vitrifies	
1,315		11		intense white
1,325	11			
1,326		12		

To calculate 100° centigrade per hour, subtract 5° centigrade.

Temperature Degrees Centigrade	British Cones	Comments
940	08	
960	07	
980	06	
1,000	05	Earthenware, biscuit and soft glazes
1,020	04	
1.040	03	
1,060	02	
1,080	01	
1,100	1	earthenware glazes
1,120	2	
1,230	7	
1,250	8	stoneware and porcelain glaze
1,280	9	
1,300	10	

British cones have generally been superseded by Orton and Harrison cones. Use British cones as above.

10 Raku

Raku is a rather more direct ceramic process. It offers a short-cut to the completed article, the characteristics of which are uniquely different from those obtained by conventional means. It involves an intimate contact with both pot and fire which has great value in developing an appreciation of ceramics. The process is both rewarding and instructional, and has much to commend itself to experienced potters and to novices, including children.

To oversimplify, perhaps, pots are biscuit fired in the normal way, glazed with low-fired glazes, decorated as required and then put directly into a pre-heated kiln. When sufficient time has elapsed to cause the glaze to melt, usually between ten and twenty minutes, the pot is removed from the kiln and fast-cooled by immersion in cold water.

To complete a Raku firing project successfully it is necessary first to consider suitable clay. After all, it is going to be subjected to considerable thermal shocks, so any body containing refractory materials would be more suitable than very smooth bodies. In fact specifically developed clays are available via suppliers which are very plastic and considerably stiffened by the addition of coarse grogs. Raku clays are readily formed into sturdy vessels or sculptural forms, will dry out without undue stress, and will withstand the sort of thermal shocks imposed by the Raku process. They are ideal for use with young children because of their 'user-friendliness' when asked to perform tasks beyond the capabilities of other less forgiving clays. It is best, therefore, to use a reliable Raku clay body.

The next stage is to produce work for firing. As a general rule, pieces should be rather chunkier than would be the case for earthenware or stoneware. The thickness of the clay could be slightly more; an increase of between twenty and fifty per cent, or from finger-thick to thumb-thick depending on the size of the item produced. Bowl forms are probably more suited to Raku than narrow-necked vessels would be, but virtually any form can be successfully fired.

There is no reason why slips or other forms of decoration should not be applied at the leatherhard state. As the character of Raku pots differs from other types, so the character of the decoration can be different too. Make it chunky, spontaneous or bold, or nothing rather than over-detailed and fiddly. The underlying philosophy is to accept 'faults' as inevitable, see them as contributing to the personality of the pot rather than detracting from it. In the same way, accidental effects, over which you have little or no control, are likely to be regarded as assets, even when they obliterate or obscure decoration consciously considered and applied to enhance the anticipated appearance of the piece.

When made and decorated as you think appropriate, the pieces should be dried out and biscuit fired in the normal way. To assist toughening, the pieces can be fired to 1,100° centigrade, or even more provided that they will accept glaze afterwards.

Glazes will have a relatively low melting point, probably in the region of between 950–1,050° centigrade. Some commercially prepared frits can be used as glazes; some require slight modifications by the addition of clay, whiting and/or flint (this is sometimes done to make them workable). Some suggested recipes are given on page 163.

As in any other type of pottery, glazes can be applied by any of the usual means, including brushing (*see* Chapter 13). Double-dipping can be useful partly for the colour and texture variation it introduces and partly because it ensures the thicker coating necessary for the Raku process. Oxides can be applied over and/or under the glaze, although any tight, precise and detailed painting is likely to be lost later.

In theory the pieces are ready for firing as soon as the glaze has dried. In practice however it is advisable to preheat the pots to dry them out thoroughly. This avoids casualties in the kiln and reduces the effects of shock when the pots are placed in the preheated kiln. I have found that if they are too hot to be picked up by hand they will probably withstand the trauma of the next step. Depending on the type and design of the kiln used these pots can be preheated by placing them on top as the kiln heats up, or in some other way making use of its heat.

As the glaze firing will be judged visually there is no need for cones. A pyrometer will give a useful and responsive reading from the chamber, the temperature of which will vary due to the opening up of the kiln which is necessary for loading and unloading. When the kiln has reached a temperature which gives a bright red heat within, the door or lid should be removed quickly, the pot placed inside, and the kiln closed up again as quickly as possible to avoid unnecessary heat loss. It is helpful in this respect to have an assistant to open and shut the kiln as you place or remove pots. If a convenient spyhole exists, a watch can be kept on the pot.

I once met an American exponent of Raku who claimed to remove red-hot pots from the kiln using only a damp tissue. Those of us blessed with non-asbestos hands, however, are better advised to use tongs to place and remove pots. These can be purchased ready-made for the job, or can possibly be created by improvisation. A pair of heat-resistant gloves which protect the forearms is also very useful.

Having placed the piece in the kiln, frequent checks to observe the state of flux will be necessary to ensure a good melt without over-firing. Glaze will tend to run, so only use sacrificial kiln bats in a Raku firing rather than risk spoiling new ones. If the colour inside the kiln has been a good bright red for ten to twenty minutes but the pot cannot be seen through the spyhole, open the kiln to check on progress. The pot should be glowing almost orange-red and the surface should have a shiny, wet look. If this is the case the pot should be removed. If not, close up and give it a little more time.

When you judge it to be ready, remove the pot by carefully grasping it with the tongs, trying not to cause unnecessary damage to the molten glaze. Some marking is inevitable, however, and has to be considered an integral part of the whole. Allow the pot to cool down naturally so that you can observe changes in the state and colour of the glaze. Alternatively, it can be placed into a metal bin containing damp dead leaves or sawdust. Having attempted to cover the pot quickly with leaves, a well-fitting lid should be placed on the bin so that smoke generated by the combustion of leaves in contact with the hot pot will be trapped within. This creates a 'reduction' atmosphere, together with oxides introduced in the decoration process and occurring from the combustion of the leaves. After about ten minutes remove the lid and use the tongs to pull the pot out. Shake off excess debris and immediately plunge the pot into a bucket of cold water. This cools it and washes off some of the deposited ash. Scrub the rest off using a nail-brush once the temperature has reduced sufficiently for the artefact to be handled.

The resulting glaze and reduced lustres are likely to be quite amazing to an inexperienced and unsuspecting observer. With a little experimentation and research you will soon develop your own procedures for adapting and adopting materials and methods to achieve your own premeditated outcomes. Like all of us who have experienced the Raku process you will be impressed by the enlightenment and insights it provides in terms of both the 'happy accident' and the firing process. The latter in particular is of such an intimate nature as to be almost an obligatory project for any would-be potter. To recap and comment on requirements for such a project:

1   Use a suitable Raku clay body to produce 'chunky' forms.
2   Biscuit fire; decorate as required. Temperature 1,050–1,100° centigrade.
3   Use low temperature glazes. Raku glazes are available commercially, or use frits to develop your own.
4   Glazes can be tested in a normal biscuit firing.
5   Preheat glazed pots.

Things needed:

1   Kiln. Some simple designs are indicated below. Use a (LPG) gas torch as burner. Or use an old electric kiln. Make sure that all power is *off* before opening. I have seen potters plunge metal tongs into a live kiln several times but have no record of their continuing good health. Top loaders lose heat rather more quickly than front loaders.
2   Rubbish bin with dead leaves.
3   Bucket of cold water.
4   Tongs.
5   Protective gloves.

The whole project can be carried out in the open air. If it is not possible to build or move a kiln outside, then at least try to keep the dustbin of leaves outside. If there is some distance between kiln and outdoors it would be advisable to have a number of small containers in which to reduce the pots. These could then be loaded and quickly removed from inside before smell and smoke becomes a problem.

This is a project suited to the back garden. It is not suitable if you only have an indoor studio/workshop.

11 The Nature of Glazes

There are a number of stages to the glazing process, whether you are starting with the development of a suitable glaze recipe or purchasing a ready-made glaze in dry powder form, which only needs to be let down into solution by the addition of water. When first embarking upon glazing and firing it is much easier to use a commercially prepared glaze but although the results will be reliable they may not be exactly what you wanted. Neither is it as much fun and as satisfying. The challenge of attempting to produce your own glazes may well be too much to resist, and the following advice is intended to assist in meeting this temptation.

I have already mentioned that clay bodies begin to bloat, blister and eventually melt when subjected to excess heat. But obviously, even where it is economically and physically possible to achieve the temperatures necessary to melt the silica contained in clay, the result would be a glaze which melted or fused at the same temperature as the body it was intended to enhance. Some means therefore need to be found to reduce effectively the overall melting point of a glaze mix so that first, it will fuse and bond to the clay body before that body is adversely affected by the heat, and second, a glasseous fusion will be achieved at temperatures possible with the available technology and without it being ridiculously uneconomic in terms of both fuel and labour.

As has been mentioned, clays bearing significant quantities of iron oxide tend to fuse, melt and eventually collapse at lower temperatures than clays containing fewer 'impurities'. If, instead of iron oxide, a metal oxide with a lower melting point is used as a fluxing agent perhaps a mix could be created which would produce this 'glass' at a convenient working temperature suitable for the ceramic process.

By medieval times British potters had developed glazes using mixtures of clays and galena (a raw oxide of lead) which fluxed when fired at around 1,000° centigrade or less. For hundreds of years these lead glazes were used, often over red bodies decorated with slips, giving rise to traditional English slipware personified by the work of the Toft brothers in the eighteenth century. Rather more recently it has been realised that the use of lead in glaze formulation has a double risk attached. Hand-mixing such glazes allows for absorption and ingestion of the metal, resulting in various forms of lead poisoning and related problems. Lead can also leach out, contaminating the contents of lead-glazed wares particularly when used for cooking or serving hot substances, exposing the consumer to similar risks.

This problem is overcome nowadays by using frits instead of raw lead oxides. These may or may not contain lead compounds but are in any case fritted, or fired, compounds. When ground down

A basis for further testing might be

frit	60%	50%	40%	parts by dry weight
clay	40%	50%	60%	parts by dry weight
	100%	100%	100%	

into powder form these provide the basic source of silica and fluxing agent, which produce a glassy substance when fired. If mixed with a clay body in the appropriate proportion a reasonable glaze can often be produced for use on earthenwares.

By first measuring out 50g of a frit and adding the same quantity of a clay body (probably the body used for the wares) a glaze mixture can be made up. By adding sufficient water to produce a solution of about single cream consistency the basic test mix can be applied to a small biscuit ware test piece and fired up to the required temperature. In the same firing, test several other mixtures made using the same ingredients in varying proportions, i.e. 40:60 or 60:40. Ensure that each test piece is clearly identified by painting its code (T1, T2 and so on) on to the ware, using a wash of manganese dioxide. Keep a record of each recipe so that accurate comparisons can be made between the various tests when they have been removed from the kiln.

These mixtures of relatively coarse minerals will require thorough mixing if tests are to be useful. All lumps must also be removed so that ingredients are evenly distributed throughout the mix. Both objectives are met if the mixes are passed through a 120 mesh sieve or lawn at least once; repeating this two or three times will obviously be better. For such small quantities, a cup sieve will be much more convenient than a normal lawn. Remember, *all* the mix has to pass through the sieve. Do not wash lumps away; they are all part of the recipe. They can be brushed over the lawn surface, using a lawn brush or a clean hog's hair oil-painting brush until nothing remains behind.

When testing any sort of new glaze mix it is better to apply and fire it on to a vertical rather than a purely horizontal surface so that the viscosity of the new recipe is checked. A glaze which tested most satisfactorily on a tile may well run almost completely off the vertical sides of thrown wares. Either throw test pieces in the form of simple egg-cups or make use of slabbed clay cut into strips and bent to form an italic L-shape.

Glaze can be applied to the upper part of the piece, providing a safety margin of unglazed ware in case of running, and an area for identification marks and abbreviated date if required. More information can be obtained about the potential glaze by applying brushstrokes of oxides over the test. These will reveal colour response and glaze stability when in contact with possible fluxing agents.

The experimental process described above and used with frits to develop earthenware glazes can be modified and used in a similar way to develop glazes for other types of wares.

It is not possible to use frits at high temperatures, due to the fryable nature

ate), quartz (a form of flint with an extremely fine crystalline structure and essentially silica, SiO_2), and clay will often produce interesting glazes. These are likely to be rather dark in colour due to the presence of iron and other metallic oxides frequently present in common rocks.

A classic glaze recipe from Daniel Rhodes is:

Cornwall Stone   85 parts (dry weight)
Whiting ($CaCO_3$)   15 parts (dry weight)

This smooth, semi-opaque glaze will craze over most bodies but is often used, applied thickly over a flat surface to give a sense of depth within the glaze. It requires temperatures of about 1,280° centigrade but small amounts of bone ash will reduce the fusion point if necessary.

Another material well worth experimenting with is wood ash. It is tempting to imagine early potters stoking wood-fired kilns, disturbing ash which might then have been carried up by the draught to be deposited on to the vitrifying surface of extremely heated clay. The ash, acting as a flux and combining with the silica and alumina in the clay body, may well have formed compounds which melted, producing a glazed surface. Once noticed, this phenomenon would have soon been recognised as a means of making compounds which would melt at required glaze temperatures.

Although ash from any wood or other vegetable matter (such as cigarette ash) can be utilised it is obviously rather difficult to obtain sufficient quantities of chemically similar material to maintain a regular and consistent supply of the raw material if required for extended use. Small batches of individual ashes can be

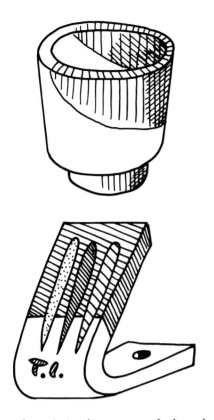

Testing glaze. A simple egg-cup or L-shaped glaze can be used to test for viscosity.

of the metal salts used. Very effective high-firing glazes can be obtained by using just a few easily obtainable natural ingredients. Granite, which is made up of mica, feldspar and quartz, has a composition very close to that of a glaze. One likely area for experiment is therefore to grind up granite into fine powder and fire it up to about 1,280° centigrade. Unless some form of grinding equipment is available, this is likely to be extremely difficult, however. Feldspar can be found in most localities and can similarly be used as the basis for developing 'found' glazes.

Combinations of other 'found' ingredients such as limestone (calcium carbon-

used to provide unique and often very beautiful glazes and this can be an extremely attractive and exciting proposition to the studio potter.

Where it is intended to use ash from a bonfire it should first be dry-sieved through a coarse screen to remove bits of charcoal and other impurities, such as nails and soot. It is then added to water to make up a thin slip and passed through a fine lawn of about 60 mesh. After settling out, excess water can be decanted off and the remains allowed to dry out either in the sun or over a kiln.

Thorough washing of the ash tends to remove not only soluble potash, which is caustic, but also other alkalis. This renders the ash less fusible in the glaze, so extended washing is not desirable. It is better to handle the ash using rubber gloves when straining and washing. Alternatively, simply sieve the ash through a 30's mesh screen and weigh it out for direct, unwashed use in the glaze recipe. Again wear rubber gloves when mixing and applying ash glazes to avoid skin irritation.

It is not possible to give recipes for wood ash glazes because the exact chemical composition of an ash will be unknown. Different woods and vegetable matters will produce differing compositions so the only way to determine a recipe for an ash glaze is by experimentation. If a reasonably large quantity of ash is available, whether from one pure source or a mixture of various ashes collected together to make up a worthwhile batch, a series of tests can be made. These can then be followed up by a working quantity of the most suitable combination of ingredients. The biggest problem, or rather source of frustration, is that if a glaze is developed which is positively wonderful, having the most desirable qualities and colour, it may never be possible to repeat it with subsequent mixes of ash. The very uniqueness of such a glaze, however, tends to make all the effort well worthwhile, and with luck the next glaze mix, although different, may have qualities to match the first.

Use the very simple model, as on page 158, to make a start on experimentation with a 50/50 mix of ash and clay, or feldspar and ash. Provided a good record is kept of all your tests, and you try to be as accurate as possible when weighing out small quantities for test purposes, there is no reason why you should not devise a wide range of permutations using, perhaps, only three ingredients. From a reasonable number of tests in only one firing it will then be possible to identify the most useful area for further investigation.

50% ash	50% clay	
50% ash		50% feldspar
50% ash	25% clay	25% feldspar
25% ash	25% clay	50% feldspar
25% ash	50% clay	25% feldspar

Proportions of glaze ingredients for testing.

If neither of the five tests suggested produces a good glaze perhaps a midway test between the two best 'failures' may provide a better result. Other ingredients can also be introduced to the tests, but change only one quantity and/or ingredient at a time so that cause and effect are always controlled and understood.

The whole concept of glaze development is fascinating, partly because although relatively few different ingredients are used, an almost inexhaustible range of results is possible and the satisfaction of producing a unique glaze is more than ample reward for the effort you make to do so.

Any glaze resulting from the suggested development processes is likely either to be transparent if it is an earthenware glaze or semi-transparent, possibly milky, if stoneware, with the possible exception of wood ash tests. In fact transparency could be considered the norm – any glaze fired to maturity will usually be clear. Many glazes, however, are cloudy or partially opaque even when containing no opacifier. If a glaze is not quite brought to fusion point it will remain matt because it is partly unmelted.

To opacify a transparent glaze, it is usual to add either tin oxide or zirconium oxide. The latter is cheaper but produces a less smooth texture than tin and is less favourable to certain oxides used to colour the glaze, or as on-glaze decoration. By increasing quantities of some metal oxides such as zinc, calcium, barium, aluminum or magnesium beyond their normal limits, clouding will occur in the glaze. By such a means semi-opaque glazes can be developed which partially reveal features underneath them. They are however very difficult to control, and if the temperature is not exactly right they will either become clear when slightly overfired, or opaque when slightly underfired. In practice it is best to add a small amount of tin oxide to a transparent glaze.

Metal oxides are used, as I have mentioned, to opacify glazes, as fluxing agents in the preparation of glaze recipes, to colour slips, and some are used as pigments for on-glaze painting. Glazes can also be stained using metal oxides as indicated in the table on page 162.

It is customary to add oxides in percentage dry weight to dry glaze. Where absolutely precise replication of the chosen test is hoped for the recipe might be:

98.5%	base glaze (dry weight)
1.5%	cobalt carbonate (dry weight)
100.0%	blue glaze

Using small quantities when testing, even the most meticulous use of laboratory scales is likely to produce different results when compared to the working recipe so exact matching is usually not possible.

To make weighing-out easier, therefore, it is often more convenient to add a nominal percentage to a 100 per cent unit of glaze:

Glaze – 100 parts
Oxide – 1.5 parts

The minute colour variation arising from an infinitesimal difference in oxide content is hardly likely to be perceptible, whereas if you are using a glaze which has already been measured out to a percentage recipe some difficulty could be experienced if precisely calculated percentages of additional oxides were required.

Using a base glaze, tests can be made up using any of the oxides mentioned below, either singly or in combinations.

METAL	% ADDED	COMMENT	COLOUR*
iron oxide (red)	1–10%	Fe_2O_3 haematite fine, stable oxide	burnt sienna yellow ochre
vanadium stain	4–10%	V_2O_5 usually with tin oxide as a prepared stain	yellow
rutile	2–10%	contains iron oxide and titanium oxide, used for texture	
manganese	2–6%	MnO_2 black dioxide powder $MnCO_3$ manganese carbonate – very fine pink powder	purple-brown to black if thick, purple response best in alkaline glazes
chrome	2–5%	Cr_2O_3 green oxide of chrome depending on glaze	red, yellow, pink, brown or green
copper oxide or carbonate	2–5%	CuO – black powder $CuCO_3$ – light green powder 1,250°C+ – volatile, influences environs, not to be used with lead oxides	1% light tint 2–3% strong colour 5% dark metallic, often black
ilmenite	1–5%	ore similar to rutile (titanium + iron)	speckled textures
iron chromate	1–3%	$FeCrO_4$ – 2% gives significant darkening of colour	grey-brown or black
nickel	½–3%	NiO green nickel oxide Ni_2O_3 black oxide	browns/greys
cobalt oxide or cobalt carbonate	½–1%	CoO black powder – very powerful $CoCO_3$ light purple powder – very fine	CoO – 0.25% will give strong blue

*Will depend on precise amount added, type of glaze and nature of atmosphere in kiln chamber. Colours indicated as a guide, in oxidation atmosphere.

Oxides commonly used in the ceramic decoration process.

Colour response will be greater when oxides are used to stain white opaque glazes containing tin oxide. The same oxides staining a transparent glaze over a red body will be lifeless and dull, resembling washes of watercolour applied on brown paper. I have deliberately omitted illustrations of coloured glaze tests because such results would not necessarily be possible in a different kiln or using a different batch of mineral ingredients, and would therefore be more misleading than helpful. If you are interested in developing coloured glazes or slips you can easily make up your own tests, using your usual clay body and the kiln you normally fire in.

GLAZE RECIPES

Earthenware

Parts by dry weight:
Transparent 1,080–1,100°C:
  lead bisilicate   71
  mineralised stone/
    Cornwall stone   13
  ball clay   12
  bentonite   4

Semi-transparent 1,080–1,100°C:
  as above plus tin oxide   3

Pewter 1,080–1,100°C:
  transparent (as above)
  + tin oxide   8
  manganese dioxide   2
  cobalt carbonate   1
  copper oxide   3

White Tin Glaze 1,100°C:
  transparent (as above)
  + tin oxide   8

Green glaze 1,100°C:
  transparent (as above)
  + copper oxide   ½
  cobalt oxide   ⅛
  manganese dioxide   1
  tin oxide   4

WIT Honey Glaze 1,100°C:
  lead bisilicate   71
  mineralised stone   13
  ball clay   12
  bentonite   4
  red iron oxide   1.5
  iron spangles   1.75
    (added *after* sieving)

Note: The transparent glaze above can be used with additions of tin oxide and

various combinations of oxides to produce a wide range of different colours and textures.

Stoneware

Cornwall stone 1,250–1,280°C:
  Cornwall stone   40.6
  china clay   15.7
  flint   26.7
  dolomite   4.5
  whiting   10.9
  zinc oxide   1.5
  bentonite   5

Tenmoku 1,250–1,280°C:
  (black breaking to red-brown):
  Cornwall stone glaze (as above)   100
  red iron oxide   15

Norman's white 1,250°C:
  feldspar, potash   50
  zinc oxide   20
  whiting   10
  tin oxide   10
  bentonite   5
(if it crazes add a little quartz to the recipe)

Matt barium glaze 1,230°C:
  feldspar, potash   37
  whiting   14
  barium carbonate   27
  china clay   13
  flint   9
(Add approximately 1 part copper carbonate for a rather fine blue. Reduces well too.)

Tenmoku 1,250–1,280°C:

nepheline syenite	85
whiting	15
china clay	10
flint	20
bentonite	3
red iron oxide	12

(If only 2–3 parts red iron oxide are added to the basic glaze a Celadon will be obtained under reduction atmosphere.)

Chun glaze 1,250–1,280°C:

feldspar	43
china clay	1
quartz	30
whiting	20
talc	4
colemanite	1
black iron oxide	1

(Will make a lovely whitish porcelain glaze by omitting black iron oxide.)

Raku Glazes

lead bisilicate frit	100
bentonite	1

(Alkaline frit + copper carbonate will give excellent turquoise blue.)

Deep green

lead bisilicate	100
bentonite	1
copper oxide	10

Pink/brown

lead bisilicate	70
china clay	3
flint	27
bentonite	2

Try:

calcium borate frit	4
china clay	1
tin oxide	¼

Or:

high alkaline frit	95
china clay	1
+ silver nitrate	3

Note: Always test recipes before mixing working quantities.

12   Decoration

The visual appearance of a pot can be modified and enhanced by variations in colour. Sometimes decorative surfaces occur directly from the making process. When modelling or welding together coils on the outside of a pot, tool or finger marks often leave coincidental patterns in relief which are sufficient in themselves to add interest to the surface. No doubt early attempts at coiling pots would have resulted in hand and tool marks being left on their surfaces. Others are known to have been made by applying soft clay to the insides of woven supports, with the result that characteristic basket patterns remain on the vessel when firing has burned away the supporting structure.

When covered with a glaze the raised bumps and edges cause the glaze to 'break', so that it is thinner on edges and thicker on flatter, smoother parts. The variation in its thickness causes differences in colour, and a transparent glaze will cause uneven surfaces to reflect light in visually exciting ways, and cause variations in tone, even though the colour will not be affected. Conscious efforts can be made, using a wide range of tools, to create an infinite variety of textural effects, and the possibilities for applying colour are enormous.

It could be said that decoration divides neatly into two compartments; texture and colour. That making pots and decorating them are also two distinct skills may also suggest itself. It is certainly true that in the industrial mass-production processes most specialist skills are practised by craftspeople who generally carry out only the one skill for which they have been specifically trained. The artist-craftsperson, however, producing studio ceramics and probably working alone or with just one or two assistants, will usually expect to be involved with all stages of production. He or she will produce work which reflects special skills and interests, so that some will highly decorate their work; others will perhaps be inclined to minimise decoration in favour of pure form and the more sculptural qualities inherent in their work.

Whether or not you consider decoration desirable, it is not absolutely necessary. As discussed elsewhere, pots intended for domestic use will almost certainly require some sort of glaze. And this is arguably a form of decoration (*see* also Design page 26). The addition of patterns, textures, symbols or images, raises a simple pot from the purely utilitarian to being purely decorative or ritualistic without reference to practical usage. The decoration process will have been carried out deliberately to improve the visual appearance of the object, recognising that its utility will not be improved, but that it will function on a different level. Decoration can also be carried out for its own sake; for therapeutic purpose, for instance, where the process is more important than the final finished appearance.

I suspect that one major problem exists, which is probably the cause of most frustration when students are initially faced with the question of decoration. The problem is, that they are rather more familiar with the results of commercial ceramics production than they are with the possibilities and qualities of studio ceramics, which is essentially different in many respects. After all, slip-cast wares *will* be smooth surfaced. If they were not they would probably not be released from the mould.

Painting and glazing results of commercial producers have to be reliable and consistent; repeat orders months or years hence depend on it. Work from one factory will not be essentially very different, either in terms of quality or appearance, from that of another.

Studio pottery, on the other hand, is not constrained by such problems as long-term consistency and certainly not by current technology. The character of an individual potter's work will reflect change and development over months if not years, and if one kilnload of pots appears to differ from another due to the vagaries of weather or to a kiln with prima donna pretensions the result may well be received as a bonus.

The important point is that studio pottery is different from commercial pottery. The character of its produce varies widely. The different rules and values have to be recognised and accepted if you are not to be constantly disappointed in the results of your efforts. In other words, use the work of studio potters as your yardstick and aim to develop a particular aspect of the craft to be your own, where you become an expert and thereby set your own standards.

TEXTURE

As I have already mentioned, texture and pattern can arise from the making process. They can be accidental, or at least unintended, but nevertheless perfectly acceptable in themselves (*see* photographs on page 97), or they can be a little more contrived. Whilst using a metal kidney tool to scrape away minor deviations to the curve when a pot is leatherhard, grog in the body of the clay can cause scratching on the surface of a vessel. If this texture is required, use a fairly coarsely grogged body such as a Raku body, scraping in varying directions to cause markings which criss-cross. These can be highlighted later either by washing pigments in the form of metal oxides into the cuts or delivering oxide to the raised surfaces only. More prominent texture could also be emphasised in a similar way, possibly with a glaze applied overall.

While removing unwanted bumps or lumps in the profile, exaggerated texture can be applied by using toothed cutting edges such as old saw blades, combs or forkends, so that two objectives are achieved in the one action. Contrasting rough and smooth can be effective, whether defined by a hard or a soft edge. One or other should be dominant, to avoid equal parts of each.

A wide variety of means can be used to impress pattern or texture on to plastic clay, even before anything has actually been made. By rolling slabs out on to coarse material an imprint will be left when the material is carefully pulled away. You may not wish to use a favourite lace tablecloth, but the principle applies to any fabric. Using a rough board, such as the cheap ply used to shutter poured concrete, its texture can be off-set on to the clay. Such slabs can be used as prefabricated sections to composite pieces, cut into tiles, or pressed on to male moulds. There is no reason why slabs should not be rolled out on loose material which, like sand, would be picked up on the surface, remaining after firing. Combustible material could be used in the same way so that indentations caused by sugar or sawdust, for example, would consequently remain in the fired clay. Any such texture could be regarded as a decorative end in itself, or could be used to add extra interest and dimension to a glazed surface.

The surface can be decorated by the application of built or modelled-on clay features. A favourite gimmick in this respect is the use of fine grass or hair-like extrusions obtained by forcing plastic clay through a kitchen sieve or a garlic press. These are stuck to the surface they are intended to decorate using slip and scoring, in the same way as any other join would be made between two pieces of clay. If it were possible to produce a definitive portfolio illustrating the full range of texture it would be undesirable in any event. Fortunately the possibility does not exist, leaving you free to experiment in any way that seems appropriate to the sort of work you produce. If you are interested in texture as a decorative medium it will be well worth setting yourself the task of developing both free textures and formal surface patterns using any simple objects as tools.

COLOUR

Returning briefly to the 'original situation', as I defined it in the introductory chapter, whereas a potter developing the craft within an early society soon recognised the possibilities of texture and pattern, opportunities to apply colour might well have been less obvious. Some pigments used in other contexts may have been found to disappear when used for ceramic purposes. Others, coloured earth pigments such as ochres, however, would have been seen to survive the ordeal by fire only to flake off the wares at a later time.

Over-simplifying the situation in the interests of brevity it would have been observed that other clay bodies of different colours were the most likely to fire on to the pot. Some would have been easily found; others, such as the pure white kaolin or china clay, would have been much more rare. Trade would have developed between potters with, and those without, desirable resources. They would also have noticed other colours staining deposits of calcium carbonate in limestone cave formations, for example, and would quickly have come to recognise the difference between vegetable and mineral pigment. It seems almost too obvious to be worth saying, but a vegetable dye such as beetroot juice will burn away totally at relatively low temperatures, whereas the dark red-brown stain of iron oxide will withstand extremely high temperatures of $1,200-1,300°$ centigrade.

Agents used in ceramics have to withstand heat, usually the same temperature as that to which the ware is subjected. There are interesting exceptions to this overall pattern, but in any event applied decoration must be durable. We all appreciate that decoration which softens or washes off when a piece is immersed in hot water is of little practical use, and would be dangerous if used as oven-to-table ware where pigments could leach out into foodstuffs, causing a risk to the consumer's health.

One of the simplest ways of introducing colour is to make use of a range of clays containing different amounts of metal oxides, most commonly red iron oxide, as impurities. Clay to be applied over another is used in slip form. It is mixed thoroughly with water, sieved through a 100 or 120 mesh lawn, and water is added so that its consistency is rather like single cream. It is applied to leatherhard clay which has been sparingly sponged over if the surface is considered to be too dry. It opens up a surprising range of possibilities with a limited range of coloured slips. Early potters would probably have been obliged to make do with one or two colours, possibly using a grey clay body decorated with red and white slips. By the addition of carefully calculated amounts of other metal oxides we can nowadays obtain a wide range of strong colours, either purchased ready prepared or developed through trial and experiment in our own workshops.

Common Oxides

Red iron oxide, as already mentioned, is frequently found in clay. It gives the characteristic terracotta colour familiar in plant pots, house bricks and a great deal of traditional earthenware.

China clay, pure white and much less commonly occurring, is used as a basis for white slips and clay bodies. A rather more expensive white pigment is tin oxide, but this is used only very selectively to modify other colour, or to opacify and whiten some glazes. Copper oxide has

been used for a very long time to produce greens. Cobalt oxide, as its name implies, gives strong blues, the Willow Pattern being perhaps a universally recognised example of its use. Manganese dioxide produces dark browns through to black.

These four, iron, copper, cobalt and manganese, provide potters with a basic palette, whether used in slips, on clay or on, in or under glazes. They are reasonably cheap, when compared to precious metals, and have a temperature tolerance wide enough to give good colour whether low or high fired. Colour will be rather more subdued at the high end of the range, but unlike softer metals they can be used at all the temperatures normally utilised in ceramics processes.

Direct Application of Oxides

Mention has already been made of the possibility of applying oxides directly to the pot either in its raw state or after biscuit firing. If it is necessary to sponge off excess oxide, then apply to biscuit ware. The oxides will not then be covered over or diluted by clay loosened and disturbed by the sponging process. The excess could be scraped away from a raw pot, causing further modification to both texture and colour. It can be an advantage to apply oxide to a raw pot because subsequent firing will, to some degree at least, fix it to the body and enable further application using glazes as vehicles, enriching surface texture and further developing the decoration. A disadvantage of applying oxides arbitrarily by any means is that there is no practical means by which quantity is measured, except by eye and experience. Where, for example, a green texturing is expected to burst up through a white glaze it may be found after firing that copper oxide was applied too liberally, causing undesirable metallic gunmetal blotches to emerge instead. Very excessive amounts of any oxide will give rise to dry, almost clinker-like eruptions in the glaze. If freely applied, textural effects can be accepted philosophically and these problems can be turned to advantage, but where carefully preconceived designs are desired, some other technique affording precise control over the concentration of colouring agents has to be sought.

Indirect Application

The Use of Slip

Oxides can be applied and amounts easily controlled if suspended in slips. These can be made from bodies of different colours, i.e. buff, terracotta or, more rarely, white. Using a limited range of colours the potter is able to ring the changes with numerous permutations. It is interesting to check on the properties of local clays, including colour before and after firing, and to imagine how the earliest potters would have searched or traded for clays, particularly the prized white bodies.

A problem experienced if different clay bodies are used as decorating slips is that of fit. Bodies shrink to different extents and at different rates when dyring out and during firing. One result of this incompatibility is that they can flake off the parent body, or be prone to cracking or chipping.

The easiest way of avoiding this is to use the parent body as the basis for the slips. Naturally, unless you are working with a white body throughout, a white slip will have to be specially formulated to fit the parent body. Following the tradition of English slipware, you could try using a red earthenware body for making pots, and use the same body to make up a dark brown or black slip by adding manganese and cobalt, a reddy-brown slip, by increasing the amount of red oxide in the parent clay, and a green or blue slip by adding copper or cobalt as appropriate. A white slip can be made up separately. To avoid buying and storing an extensive range of raw materials it may be more convenient to purchase ready-to-use slips. These are developed to suit specific bodies recommended and supplied by Potterycrafts Ltd. for example.

Whether purchasing ready-made slip or making up your own the range of possibilities has been extensively widened, particularly over the past few years. If you wish to enjoy the satisfaction of making up your own slips you will find that adding the four basic oxides in light and dark slips will radically extend the permutations, using this delightfully simple method of decoration.

The degree of control over final colour will also be enhanced. In order to arrive, for example, at a satisfactory blue slip, tests will have to be made using varying amounts of oxide added to fixed amounts of dry clay by weight. Tests can be carried out using different bodies too, each of which will affect or modify the eventual colour.

In percentage terms a recipe for testing could be made up as follows:

96% red clay powder (dry weight)
4% cobalt oxide (dry weight)

By adjusting the amount of cobalt oxide

by one or two steps either way a range of possibilities can be tested at the same time:

Red clay powder   98% 97% 96% 95% 94%
Cobalt oxide   2%   3%   4% 5%   6%

As copper and cobalt oxides tend to be powerful colouring agents it is sometimes convenient to substitute their carbonates. Also, the oxides are both black in colour, whereas cobalt carbonate is a lilac-pink colour and copper carbonate a powdery green. This is a useful aid to identification if labels are lost, and in decorating, when it would be extremely difficult to visualise eventual outcomes when looking at marks which are indistinguishable from one another.

As test ingredients will have to be weighed out in very small quantities, probably amounting in each test to 2oz (50g) total, a sensitive and accurate laboratory scale is necessary. The object of testing, after all, is not just to try out new recipes, but to economise by not having to risk producing a large quantity of an unwanted colour. The same is also true for glaze testing which is discussed on page 158.

Slips are applied when the pot is still damp, not more than leatherhard. Most of the possibilities of slip decoration can be explored by utilising simple projects such as tile-making or using a press-dish mould as described earlier (*see* page 70). Slips can be painted on, although there is sometimes a problem where the parent body colour intermixes with brushed-on slips, causing an uneven brush-mark pat-

Pouring.

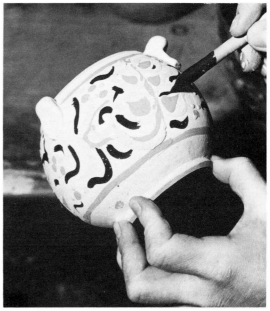

Dipping a pot. The maximum immersion is two seconds.

Brushing on coloured glazes over a base glaze.

tern to break through. Where an even coat is required, it is advisable to pour on the slip and then pour off the excess. In the case of vertical surfaces, the sides of mugs for example, the pot should be briefly immersed to the required depth so that an even deposit of slip coats the surface. A covering can be given in the required colour, leaving some areas in the original body colour; inside, or foot, for example, and this in turn can be regarded as the starting point for further decoration.

Slipware is mainly known for its characteristic trailed-on decoration as personified by the work of the Toft brothers. Slip can be poured from specially adapted spoon or jug-like containers similar to those used for batik work on fabric, or (more commonly) squeezed from rubber bulbs through nozzles which allow precise drawing of designs

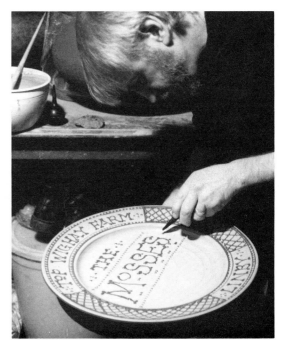

Sliptrailing on a large plate.

on to the base slip. These bulbs, or slip-trailers, can be purchased from suppliers or you can use washing-up liquid bottles and other plastic containers with narrow nozzles. Slip could even be squeezed out of the perforated finger of a rubber glove, although I find that the tool made specifically for the job usually handles better than rather clumsy alternatives. To repeat the necessary process so far:

1   Ensure that the pot has stiffened sufficiently, i.e. is leatherhard.
2   If it is drying on the surface, damp it by sponging to improve adhesive qualities.
3   Apply background slip (if required) and allow to stand until the surface loses its shine. If feathering is intended, trail the pot in wet slip.
4   The decoration can now be carried out, trailing directly on to the damp surface already prepared.

Rudimentary points to bear in mind when trailing are:

(a)   Completely fill the slip trailer to exclude air from the bulb, refilling well before it is empty.
(b)   At the end of each 'trail' or gesture, ensure that air is not inadvertently sucked up into the container. Air bubbles can cause problems if allowed to be ejected under pressure. The spitting emission at the nozzle end can splatter slip over a pristine, and usually neat, complete design, totally ruining what had been considered up to that point the best piece of work you had achieved to date. So keep the bulb as full as possible, excluding air accidentally inhaled by inverting the bulb and gently squeezing until slip just dribbles from the nozzle.

Wiping glaze off to prevent sticking.

(c)   Clean the nozzle after each gesture to prevent unwanted drips.
(d)   When moving from one section of the design to another try to keep the trailer off the work (as per (c) above).

The main attraction of slip decoration is that it is virtually impossible to make a mistake. As the design grows, much as an oil-painting develops, it can be modified. A misplaced blob can be turned to advantage by working into it with other colours, or incorporating it into the design so that the overall effect is of richness and spontaneity. And if the result is totally unacceptable it can, in extreme cases, be wiped off using a large natural sponge. It is important to remember, however, that slips are wet and lose water to the pot, and excessive wetting could cause a pot to collapse or split. Be inventive *and* philosophical, therefore, and accept the technique for what it is – delightfully direct and somewhat imprecise.

Sgraffito

As its name implies, this technique is concerned with scratching. If a contrasting slip is applied to a pot and allowed to dry, totally or just beyond the leatherhard state, a great opportunity exists for creating a sophisticated decoration by carving or scratching through it to reveal the colour of the parent body. Decoration can be entirely sgraffitoed or can be combined with trailing. I prefer to carve through a cheesy layer of slip so that edges remain crisp and clean. When slip has dried out completely it is brittle and has a tendency to chip, particularly if the tool is not sharp enough, or if it is used with too much vigour. Its major advantage is that, unlike trailing, there is a relatively dry surface on which to sketch out the design lightly as described below. Sgraffito tools can be purchased specially made for the purpose, but all manner of items can be used instead as long as they are comfortable to hold and easy to use. Lino cutting tools, very small screwdrivers, or even one half of an old pair of small scissors would be suitable. These or other items might well make marks of different character, extending the vocabulary beyond the simple fine line, and require experiment and ingenuity to enrich the design in a variety of different ways.

Leatherhard wares are fragile at the best of times; when carving it is well to support the area to be worked from the back if possible. Plates can be supported on bats, taking care not to lean on rims, and where possible work with one hand carving, the other inside or behind, when working on hollow ware.

There are two ways of transferring designs on to the slipped surface, based on the same principle. The first requirement is a design. Original art work can be drawn and painted, to create an 'artist's impression' of the finished item, or design or pattern can be worked up directly on to the detail paper used to transfer the design to the ware.

Going straight on to the latter, proceed as follows. Use a sketch book or drawing board with clean white paper. Cover the blank sheet with detail or tracing paper. Detail paper is stronger, allowing a great deal of modification without damage. Graphic designers and architects use it, among others, and it can be obtained from good art or drawing-office supply shops.

Use a reasonably soft pencil which is easy to rub out if necessary, say a 2B, and mark out the exact size of the required area to be decorated. Use drawing instruments as necessary. Then very lightly rough in the basic idea, gradually tightening it up until you are satisfied that you have enough information to guide you in the carving process.

Turn the detail paper over and retrace the design on its reverse side using a soft pencil, such as 4B or 6B, to deposit graphite liberally on to the paper.

The detail paper has now been converted into a sort of carbon sheet. It is now placed carefully in position on the pot, enabling the design to be transferred, by off-set printing really, to the pot.

Stencilling on lettering prior to sgraffito.

Sgraffito – cutting through slip to reveal the colour of the body.

Gently but firmly trace over the design using a B or HB pencil, pressing sufficiently on to the paper to deposit graphite on the pot, repeating your design exactly. The design can now be carved into the clay, any remaining graphite being burned off in the firing.

The alternative is to use a pin to prick through the detail paper, eventually joining up the dots, either with a soft pencil, some sort of vegetable dye, painted on lightly, or working direct with the sgraffito tool.

Use a fine point with which to make your first incision, widening the marks appropriately and progressively with larger tools later, creating interesting relationships between different types of line – straight, curved, wide, narrow, hard, soft, and so on. Broad areas can be treated to dotting, pricking or hatching, again extending the variety of and hence the visual effect of the finished design.

If a white slip is used on a red body and the whole covered with a honey glaze the result will be a rich honey-tinted cream with rich reddish-brown detail, and a wonderfully warm sparkle. More details about glaze will be included in the appropriate chapter, and some slip recipes will be given below.

In addition to the above form of sgraffito, the opposite effect can be achieved using similar techniques. In this instance the design with which you wish to decorate your pot must be scratched, fairly deeply, into its surface. You then fill these grooved areas with slip, dabbing the slip in such a way as not to disturb the underlying clay. The pot is then left to dry out. Once it is completely dry you then scrape away the spare surface slip, using a steel kidney, to reveal the slip-filled recesses of your design.

Variations

Having discussed the slip decorator's options of putting on and carving off slip, brief mention should be made of a few variations to these which you may feel inclined to develop in your own way.

1   Slip (or oxides or glazes, for that matter) can be applied by spraying or splattering. Use a toothbrush or nail-brush to flick pigment from it by dragging a finger or tool across the ends of the pigment-loaded bristles, projecting oxide towards the surface to be decorated.
2   Use leaves, or torn or cut paper patterns to act as masks or stencils. Splatter, pour or paint slips, depositing colour on to uncovered areas.
3   As 2 above but also emphasise texture by carefully impressing a stencil object into the soft clay. (Note: remove stencils before slip dries to avoid the risk of chipping. Use a needle or compass point to lift stencils up from beneath slip, to avoid finger marks.)
4   Combing, scratching into wet slips, using a variety of tools, fingers, etc.

In the interests of clarity it is necessary to compartmentalise techniques, with the result that there may be a tendency to maintain clear cut divisions and inappropriate barriers. There is no reason why they should not be combined or modified to suit personal needs. A unique strength of the craft is its potential for individual development and expression, so that in this respect the potter is constrained by very few technical or aesthetic conventions. Familiarity with contemporary studio ceramics will reveal a wealth of adaptation, innovation and broken 'rules' which have greatly extended and enriched the potter's vocabulary.

In an attempt to economise on storage space and in financial terms, particularly where slips are only infrequently required, it is possible to purchase powdered white and red earthenware bodies in relatively small amounts, using them as bases for coloured slips. The simplified weighing out and mixing process can easily be carried out and understood by quite young potters and this will certainly outweigh any slight loss in quality.

It will be found that slips, when applied, have colours bearing no real resemblance to their descriptions, and in this respect they are similar to glazes. After an initial biscuit firing, colour will be a little more apparent, but to develop fully they require glazing. Traditionally a lead-based transparent glaze would have been used, suffusing the colours with a characteristic warm honey colour (*see* Chapter 11 on glazes). We can either use a transparent glaze which will allow white to remain unaffected and other colours unmellowed by the iron oxide 'wash', or the same glaze can be converted to a honey glaze by the addition of a little red iron oxide.

Body Stains

Whereas coloured slips cover, as it were, a neutral body, it is possible to colour bodies throughout. After all, red clay has its characteristic terracotta colour due to the red iron oxide picked up as an impurity during its formation. By adding quantities of any other oxides, bodies can be coloured as required. However, first a few words of caution. Some oxides are relatively cheap if used as pigments in slips, glazes, or as over or under-glaze paints, but they become prohibitively expensive when used to colour large quantities of clay. Prepared body stains or under-glaze colours used to do the same job would be even more costly. As a general rule, use a light or white body. If porcelain is used you will find that small amounts of body can be stretched to make quite a lot of pot. Metal oxides added to a body can act, to a greater or lesser degree, as fluxes (*see* Glossary page 185) when the clay is fired. Do, therefore, test carefully before committing your precious wares to the fire.

Stained bodies can be used simply to provide a desired colour overall. Pieces or strips of different colours can be pressed, folded or wedged together to produce deliberate or arbitrary colour changes, some examples of which appear among the colour plates.

ON-GLAZE PAINTING

Pigments in the form of metal oxides can be painted on top of a glaze. Majolica and Faience wares have been developed to a high level in their appropriate geographical locations, and reflect the brilliance and excellence of both the colour response and the brush-work possible when using simple oxides.

After thorough drying and biscuit firing, wares are coated with (usually) an opaque white glaze. Decoration is then applied direct to the unfired surface of the glaze, building up the design using bold brush strokes to suggest rather than slavishly copy or repeat natural forms and patterns.

Designing

Decoration can be built up step-by-step, making intuitive responses to what has already been done, relating marks or areas of one colour to that of another. Alternatively, a design can be developed on paper and transferred when ideas have been tried and tested. The problem here is that what is possible using a pencil, eraser and paint on paper will not always work in the same way on a pot, particularly when covered with unfired glaze. So whatever means are used to plan out the initial idea, it has then to be translated into 'on-glaze'. In other words, the vocabulary of on-glaze has to be used. There are four colours available for this work, which can be applied thickly or thinly to exploit tonal ranges. Brushes and other means by which colour can be applied, each with their own characteristic qualities, offer further areas of exploration.

As a general guide to individual experimentation, the following may be helpful.

Manganese dioxide Dark browns, purplish with alkaline glazes. Use first in thin pencilled lines to establish the structure of the design. Used as a 'clothesline' upon which to hang the rest of the design.

Red iron oxide Red-browns down to yellow ochre when applied thinly. Can be used boldly, and is not as strong as others, so thickness is not critical.

Cobalt oxide/carbonate Blues. Very strong – use thinly. Is very effective used monochromatically (as per Willow Pattern).

Copper oxide/carbonate Greens. Very strong, also volatile. Tends to 'bleed out',

blurring edges. Can affect colour of adjacent pots in kiln. Can cause glaze to run on vertical surfaces. Avoid large, broad bands, or quantities near foot of pot.

It is always useful to avoid the literal. Use a colour because of its relationship with other colours; because it looks right in a particular position and in a particular strength or amount. Grass may be green, sky can be blue, but these limiting concepts of colour should not be allowed to affect your designs adversely.

The major problem is that the surface to be decorated is dry and powdery. Pigment *has* to be applied in a lively and spontaneous manner in order not to drag off dry glaze or overload the surface with oxides. This begs the question, how thick should the oxide be applied? There really is no precise answer to this, except to say that variations in colour intensity are characteristic of the technique. Experience helps you decide this, as does a test. Paint a brush-stroke of pigment mixed with water on to old newspaper – if it is possible to read the print through the oxide it is probably not too thick. Needless to say, this is a very imprecise judgement, being at best a rough indication of excessive thickness or over-dilution.

Practice

The powdery surface to be decorated offers a very real challenge to the would-be on-glaze painter. Mistakes cannot be erased; the only option open being to wash off all the glaze and start again, after the pot has dried out sufficiently to accept glaze once more. It can be helpful to practise first on blotting paper, which is almost as difficult to paint on, and it is certainly essential to think in terms of 'one-stroke' techniques. A 'vocabulary' of brush strokes, sponge imprints and so on should be developed so that the design can literally be built up in stages. Explore the variations possible using blotting paper or newspaper with iron oxide or, cheaper still, red clay in the form of thin slip.

The problem posed by the dry, unfired glaze surface can be solved by subjecting the ware to a 'hardening on' firing. Pots to be on-glaze painted are glazed then fired to a temperature high enough to harden the surface of the glaze without causing it to melt. Depending on the glaze, this would probably be at about 950–1,000° centigrade. The resulting surface is hard but still porous, and very much easier to decorate. Mistakes, however, still cannot be erased; and the cost of an additional firing and all the handling that this involves usually makes it impractical in a school or college setting. Where an individual potter chooses to establish the practice in his or her own workshop, judgements will have been made as to the relative cost of firing, for example, as against savings in terms of spoilt pots and time.

As most studio potters produce one-offs or a range of relatively simply decorated repetition domestic ware, the tendency is to work with, and respond to, limitations rather than to eradicate them. In this respect potters will refer to qualities such as 'lively', 'spontaneous', 'exciting' rather than 'precise', 'identical' or 'consistent'.

On-glaze decoration is a method which can be applied to any type of ware. Academic distinctions apart, the intention is simply to apply oxides on top of an unfired glaze. Colour response will be at its brightest at the lower end of the glaze temperature range and when used on a white ground. The latter could be achieved by the use of a classic white tin glaze, opaque white or off-white glaze maturing at higher temperatures, or could arise from the use of a white body or slip under a transparent glaze. Oxides can be applied over coloured glazes, but obviously the resulting colour will be influenced by background in the same way that washes of water-colour paint are less vibrant when used on dark toned papers.

UNDER-GLAZE PAINTING

Where a light coloured body or slip is used, oxides can be painted directly on to the biscuit ware and glazed over afterwards. The result is a more translucent colour than would be obtained by application over the glaze; however, an opaque glaze will probably obliterate thin coatings completely. If this mode of decoration is envisaged it would probably be worth making up a semi-opaque, milky glaze as suggested elsewhere. A wide range of underglaze colours are available, but it is worth testing firing-temperature claims before putting them to serious use.

Lustres and Enamels

Delving into illustrated literature concerned with the history of pottery, or making a visit to a museum housing a reasonable collection of ceramics, will suggest, in the richness and variety of ceramic decoration, that there must be other techniques in addition to those suggested above. Such is indeed the case, but it would be impossible to cover the whole range of possibilities adequately in a book such as this. To mention sophisticated techniques in passing might be considered inappropriate, but both lustre and enamel must be mentioned, at least briefly, to indicate other areas of further enquiry rather than to provide in-depth cover of specific skills.

As I mentioned, some metal oxides can withstand ceramic temperatures; others cannot. Soft metals such as gold and silver cannot be fired at glaze temperatures but can be fired on to ware at temperatures still high enough to make them durable. Other oxides when mixed with glasseous frits can also be fired on. These two methods require different firing temperatures, enamels being higher fired than lustres. The table on page 155 indicates these.

RECIPES FOR COLOURED SLIPS

White

1   Use 100% white earthenware body – test for compatibility.

2   Ball clay   85–88 parts.
Body   15–12 parts.
3   Feldspar (potash)   32 parts.
China clay   3½ parts.
Ball clay   10½ parts.

Brown

Red earthenware body   8 parts.
Feldspar (potash)   1 part.
China clay   ½ part.
Red iron oxide   ½ part to enrich colour.

Green

Green under honey glaze – blue under transparent.
Ball clay   80 parts.
Body   10 parts.
Cobalt carbonate   1 part.
Green for transparent glaze – substitute cobalt for copper carbonate.

Black

Body   8 parts.
Feldspar (potash)   1 part.
China clay   ½ part.
Manganese dioxide   ½ part.
Red iron oxide   1½ parts.

13 Mixing and Applying Glazes

MIXING

Commercially prepared glazes and most raw materials are supplied sufficiently finely ground to pass through a 200 mesh lawn. In fact some commercially prepared glazes can be used without further preparation if the necessary water is added, the mix allowed to soak at least overnight and then thoroughly stirred. As the stirring is likely to take longer than passing the glaze through a 100 sieve, however, and the subsequent suspension more evenly distributed, it is not usually worth attempting to shortcut the preparation process. Pass the mix through a sieve two or three times to ensure that all ingredients, particularly in a workshop glaze containing added metal oxides, are dispersed evenly throughout the mix.

Amounts of water to be added to dry mixes will vary according to the glaze. As a rough general guide add sufficient water to allow the glaze to pass through the 100 sieve without too much difficulty. After the first sieving stir the mix by hand to check consistency. If it is rather like a double cream it will probably be about right. After the third sieving the mix can be diluted to about single cream consistency. When a hand is dipped in and immediately withdrawn and flicked once, the glaze should cover the fingernails, breaking to reveal the centres of the nails while clogging the quicks. When a piece of biscuit ware is dipped quickly in and out of the bucket and allowed to dry, it should have a coating of glaze about as thick as a thumbnail or $\frac{1}{32}$nd of an inch.

When glazes have been prepared ready for use, they have a tendency to settle out. This is very useful when too much water has inadvertantly been added. Once the glaze has settled, excess water can be decanted off very easily. The tendency to settle is of course stronger for the heavier ingredients of a glaze. It is therefore advisable to keep the glaze in total suspension when in use by frequent stirring. An addition of about one per cent of bentonite to the recipe will assist in keeping the mixture in suspension.

APPLYING

Glaze can be applied to ware by painting, pouring, dipping or spraying. For small modelled forms, especially if different coloured glazes are to be applied, painting will suffice. Bear in mind that biscuit ware is 'hot'. That is to say, it absorbs moisture rapidly causing 'drag' to occur whereby the brush seems to stick and pull. It is probably best to apply glaze in single brush strokes or blobs, building up the surface almost by modelling rather

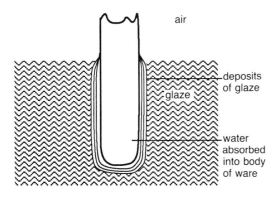

Dipping, the most convenient way of applying glaze.

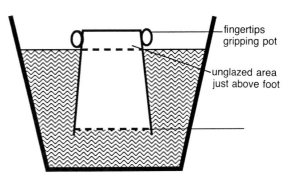

Dipping a beaker. Air trapped inside the pot prevents the glaze level from rising inside for more than about ¼–½in (0.6–1cm).

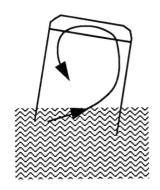

If the pot is tipped, glaze will enter and the inside of the pot can be fully glazed by causing a wave effect inside the pot.

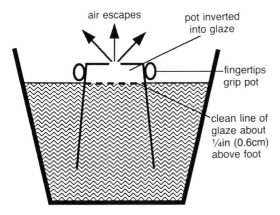

Dipping a planter or flowerpot. The hole in the foot allows the air to escape and the level of glaze to rise on the inside of the pot.

than by attempting to brush out the glaze. It will not flow like a household paint and on larger areas it will produce an uneven, textured surface which is usually rather unattractive.

Dipping

Dipping is the quickest and most convenient means of applying glaze for pots which can be easily held in the hand or in a glazing claw. By lowering an inverted piece into the glaze a neat high tide mark is left where the pot is glazed below, and remains unglazed at the foot. This method avoids the need to clean up the foot after glazing, or the need for stilts or spurs when firing. Where it is necessary to glaze the inside this should be done by pouring, filling and emptying with glaze quickly, before dipping the outside.

Using some form of glazing claw, a pot can be dipped so that inside and outside are glazed at the same time. In this case the foot will have to be wiped completely clean of glaze, or the pot fired on a spur to prevent it sticking to the kiln shelf.

With practise small pots, such as mugs, can be glazed inside and out in one overall action while keeping the foot

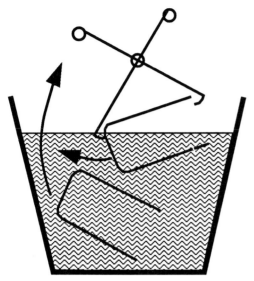

A glazing claw allows the whole pot to be glazed. Lower the pot in base-first, tilted to allow glaze to flow inside. Then lift out upside-down to drain off glaze.

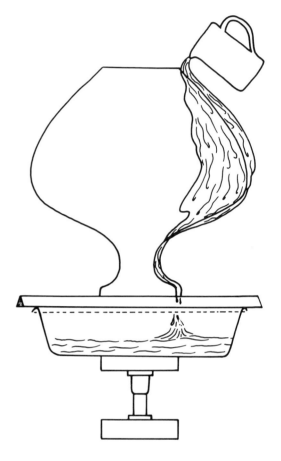

Glazing a pot by pouring. Remember to shake out excess glaze before it dries to ensure a smooth finish.

clear of glaze. Hold the pot firmly by the foot using thumb and finger tips. Invert the pot and lower it quickly into the glaze to the required depth. Tilt the pot a little so that some glaze is admitted to the inside, and firmly jerk the pot upwards, downwards and up out of the glaze, moving it quickly so that a sort of tidal wave splashes glaze right up into the bottom of the vessel. The best way to practise this is by using a glass tumbler when washing up or using glaze so that the wave effect can be seen as it happens. It is a flick of the wrist job which, used carefully, can save time in handling a number of pots and is much quicker and more convenient.

Pouring

Wares which, as a consequence of size or shape, cannot easily be dipped can usually be glazed by pouring. Glaze the

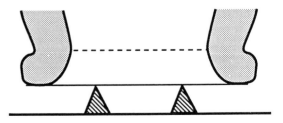

The foot of the pot supported on wooden laths for minimal contact whilst glazing.

inside if necessary by partially filling and then pouring off the glaze while turning the vessel to ensure a complete covering of the inside. While inverted, firmly shake out excess glaze before it dries. While the vessel is drying off, the next stage can be prepared. Particularly if the pot to be glazed is very large, first place a banding wheel (*see* opposite) on the floor. Place a sufficiently large bowl or similar receptacle on the wheel. Then put into place two slats of wood strong enough to carry the weight of the pot. Ideally these should be triangular in cross-section. The pot can now be stood upside-down on the slats, over the bowl, so that glaze poured over it will be collected rather than poured on to the floor.

When the pot is set up ready for glazing, check first that you have plenty of glaze within easy reach of your jug and second that you can pour with one hand while carefully turning the pot with the other, using the foot of the pot.

Pour the glaze steadily but quickly, turning the pot to coat it all over. Do not attempt to coat carefully only a single layer. Work fast and literally wash on glaze while washing off excess thickness before it has a chance to dry. Use plenty of glaze, quickly, for an even coating. If varying thicknesses are required, slow up accordingly, depositing thin or thick glaze by accident or by design. Further partial pourings of other glaze could be applied, giving added interest to texture and colour, but clean up and save each glaze as you go, otherwise a bowlful of intermixed glaze will result.

Incidentally, odd ends of glazes, if they are all usually fired to the same temperature, can be mixed together in one container. Quantity is built up making sufficient to glaze the insides of vessels where exact colour is not critical. Use of such 'counter' glazes makes economical sense and avoids the need for endless small lidded containers, whose labels have fallen off, which have to be stored somewhere.

When dealing with large or awkward shapes, there is no need always to dip or pour in one go. In fact it can be advantageous to dip one side or part, allowing it to dry before applying glaze to the other side. A double dipped region can often provide a lively contrast to other areas of glaze and, as has already been mentioned, different glazes can also be applied, giving rise to a rich range of glaze possibilities.

Use ingenuity and imagination to overcome problems both technical and aesthetic. If you don't have a plastic bowl big enough to catch the flow off, maybe a dustbin lid suitably supported will suffice. If you have never used a combination of two glazes before it could be worth taking a chance.

Spray Application

Pouring glaze can be a messy process and possibly rather wasteful when articles are large and of extremely eccentric shape. In such instances it can be much more convenient to apply glaze by spraying. As the cost of equipment can be prohibitive to the studio potter who might only make use of it on rare occasions I will not devote a lot of space to this method. To spray properly it is necessary to have a reasonably powerful compressor. If spraying in a workshop, a spray booth which extracts glaze particles safely is also necessary. We have an obsolete gun and compressor which we use outdoors in fine weather if absolutely necessary, but we consider a bona fide spray shop to be both undesirable and economically unviable.

Stand the piece to be sprayed on a banding wheel placed on a stool or directly on the lawn so that it can easily be turned while being sprayed. Use a mask and goggles to protect yourself from glaze particles. Keep the spray gun and pot moving and spray in bursts to build up an even coating. Most guns will deliver a fine mist at about one foot (30cm) from the object. If held too close, glaze will be applied too thickly and will run before it dries. If the gun is held too far away, particles of glaze will be too widely dispersed and will be dry. Practise spraying on old newspaper at first. Remember to spray up or down under overhangs and watch out for 'shadows' caused by protuberances such as knobs or handles. Keep upwind of the object to be sprayed, and choose a day when there is little or no wind. If you can use old newspaper or an old sheet as a backdrop to the spray area you will avoid unnecessary dispersal and pollution by the glaze and make it easier to clean up afterwards.

Glaze application is relatively easy. The simple methods are the cheapest and often the most convenient. Remember:

1   Keep glazes in suspension by frequent stirring. Use your hand so that you can feel the consistency.
2   Whichever means you use, be quick.
3   Glazed feet require spurs or stilts when firing.
4   Wipe foot clean of glaze. No trace should be left.
5   Clean off glaze about one quarter up from the foot to allow movement of the glaze in the kiln.
6   Avoid touching the glaze until it is completely dry – it will not take long.

Glossary

Absorption Soaking up of water by a clay body.

Agate ware Stratified mixture of different coloured clay bodies.

Alkalies Obtained from salts, spars, silicates and ashes used to vitrify glazes and bodies. Compounds of sodium and potassium, and often magnesia and lime.

Ball clay A highly plastic, fine-grained clay usually combined with other less plastic clays.

Bat A plaster or wooden slab or disc on which wares are produced or dried.

Batwash Mixture of infusible minerals painted on to shelves to prevent pots sticking during firing.

Bag/bag wall Firebrick wall to divert flame from direct contact with wares.

Bentonite An extremely fine clay. Use 1–2 per cent in a glaze to aid suspension.

Biscuit/bisque Unglazed clay fired once at a low temperature, usually between 1,000° centigrade and 1,100° centigrade. Body remains porous.

Bloating Blisters in clay due to over-firing.

Body Refers to prepared clay. Usually mixtures of clays with different characteristics.

Borax Powerful frit used in many glazes.

Carbon soak Kiln temperature held at about 900° centigrade for thirty minutes or more to facilitate oxidation.

Calcine Carbon dioxide and chemical water driven off by subjecting ceramic substance to moderate heat, 350–700° centigrade.

Calipers A tool used to measure internal or external diameter of cylinders.

Carbon dioxide Liberated in the form of bubbles erupting through the melting surface of a glaze. Can cause blisters. Causes decomposition of carbonates.

Casting The pouring of liquid clay into plaster moulds to make wares.

Ceramic fibre Highly efficient, lightweight insulating material. Resembles glass fibre.

Celadon Name of stoneware glaze with a green colour resulting from reduction of iron oxide in the glaze recipe.

Chalk Calcium carbonate, marble, limestone or whiting. For glaze-making purposes all are approximately the same thing. Are used as fluxing agents in high-fired glazes.

Chatter A blunt or wrongly held turning tool will vibrate against a leatherhard pot during turning.

Chemical water Water combined with alumina and silica to form theoretical clay molecule.

China clay China clay, kaolin or alumina. Pure white firing clay used for porcelain or opacifying glazes. Molecular formula: $Al_2O_3.2SiO_2.2H_2O$.

Chun glaze A thick opalescent high temperature glaze.

Clay Decomposed feldspathic rock which is uniquely plastic so it can be formed into an endless range of forms.

Coiling An ancient and effective method of building large pots.

Combing The use of a blunt-toothed comb to decorate the wet surface of a pot.

Cones Pyrometric cones measure heat-work done.

Cornish stone Natural granite containing a large amount of feldspar. Most frequently used raw flux for stoneware glazes, and essential in porcelain bodies.

Crackle Intentional crazing of a glaze surface for decorative purposes.

Crazing An unintentional faulty crackling of a glaze.

Crystallisation When cooled slowly, some glazes will develop crystal formations.

Dampers In kiln flues, can be adjusted to control draught and atmosphere.

Dipping Immersion of pots into slip or glaze.

Down draught kilns In which the arrangement of burners and flue cause the flames to travel downwards through the ware before exiting up the chimney.

Drawing Unpacking a kiln.

Dunting Inrushing cold air causes pots to crack.

Earthenware Red or white clay body of a porous nature. Optimum firing temperature of 1,150° centigrade.

Enamels Actually low-firing glazes applied over higher firing glaze to introduce bright colour to decoration.

Engobes Slips.

Extrusion A process by which solid bricks and hollow pipe-sections can be made by forcing clay through a die of an appropriate shape.

Faience Loosely used to describe glazed earthenware but specifically refers to tin-enamelled earthenware produced in Faenza, Italy.

Feldspar Rectilinear opaque white crystals found in granite. Melts at between 1,200° centigrade and 1,300° centigrade. Important fluxing agent in glaze recipes.

Fettling Smoothing or finishing the surface of leatherhard clay.

Flaking Raw slips or glazes scale off during drying due to expansion/contraction incompatibility. Can also be caused by grease or dust on glazed biscuit wares.

Flint Is calcined and finely ground, and added to glazes and bodies to introduce silica to the mix.

Flux Any material which will assist vitrification: the lowest melting compound in glaze recipes.

Fluxing agents Can be bone or wood ash, borax or lead in the forms of frits, or lime. These combine chemically with more refractory substances such as clay and silica, effecting vitrification.

Frits Glasses composed of silica and alkaline salts which are melted and finely ground. Used to make lead salts non-toxic or glazes insoluble.

Galena Lead sulphide. Lead bearing ore, finely ground and used for production of English slipware.

Glaze A surface coating of glass which seals porous bodies. Often decorative.

Glost firing Glaze firing. Used to mature glazes so that they fuse on to the body. Temperatures vary according to the type of glaze.

Granite A common igneous rock containing mica, quartz and feldspar. Most clays originate from the decomposition of its feldspar.

Greenware Unfired wares.

Grog Crushed or ground refractory material, usually fired fireclays, which reduces shrinkage or warping. Sometimes added to give texture.

Hard paste porcelain Made of china clay, Cornish stone or feldspar and other natural minerals, and matured at over 1,300° centigrade.

Homogeneous Of the same, uniform,

consistency. In clay, a body with even consistency and texture, containing no foreign bodies, lumps or air bubbles.

Impermeability When ceramics have been vitrified they are non-porous.

Incise To cut surface designs into ware as a form of decoration.

Kaolin China clay.

Kneading Working clay by hand to homogenise it ready for use.

Lawn/screen Gauzes of bronze wire used for sieving glazes and slips.

Leatherhard When clay loses moisture and plasticity it becomes cheese or leatherhard. It will bend without cracking, can be cut easily, and joined with slip, but will retain a given shape.

Lug Knob or other kind of protuberance used as a handle.

Lustre Decoration applied over mature glaze in the form of metals suspended in liquid to form a skin over the glaze. Subsequently fired on at low temperature, often reduced, as in Raku.

Magnetic iron/iron spangles (Fe_3O_4) Is more resistant to high temperature than red iron oxide (Fe_2O_3). Can be used to add 'sparkle' to glazes.

Majolica White tin glazed earthenware decorated with on-glaze enamels or oxides.

Marbled ware Superimposition of coloured slips on leatherhard pots and subsequent jogging or shaking to cause the colours to intermix arbitrarily.

Matt glazes Have a dull surface which do not reflect light.

Neutral Atmosphere in a kiln chamber which is midway between oxidising and reducing (*see* Reduction).

Open firing Where fire plays directly upon exposed wares.

Overglaze/enamel painting Decorating a hard glaze with oxides which adhere to the surface due to added proportions of soft flux.

Oxidation The firing of a kiln so that sufficient oxygen is available for complete combustion. Oxides in clay and glazes will give their normal colours.

Placing Packing wares into a kiln.

Plaster of Paris Gypsum, calcium sulphate or sulphate of lime. When mixed with water (approximately 5lb/2.3kg plaster to 3½ pints/2 l water) and mixed, it sets hard. Used for casting moulds.

Plasticity The unique property of clay which allows it to be modelled and reworked.

Porcelain Applies to pottery which is white, translucent and high-fired – true porcelain at over 1,300° centigrade.

Pottery Any artefact made of clay which has undergone chemical changes produced by heat over 600° centrigrade.

Primary clay Clays which are direct derivatives of feldspars, such as china clay. Found in place of origin.

Pug mills In effect oversize mincing machines which use a wormscrew principle to compress, churn and mix clay.

Pyrometer Used to indicate the precise temperature inside a kiln as measured by a thermocouple.

Raku Dramatic method of producing ceramic wares based on Japanese tea ceremony and named after the great tea master Seno-no-Rikyu.

Reduction Atmosphere in a kiln where combustion is incomplete or smoky due to restricted oxygen supply. Achieved by using dampers or increasing supply of fuel to excess; allows carbon fuel to draw oxygen from glazes and bodies and changes colour of some metal oxides, for example, copper oxide gives an ox blood red under reduction, green in oxidation.

Refractory Ceramic materials already

subjected to high firing, or by nature unaffected by proposed firing temperatures.

Rib   A tool, usually wooden, used for throwing.

Salt glaze   Salt (sodium chloride) introduced to a stoneware kiln vapourises and combines with silica to form a thin glaze often with characteristic 'orange peel' texture.

Secondary clays   Clays that have been carried from their site of origin to be deposited elsewhere. These usually pick up impurities such as iron oxide, alkalies, lime and magnesia. Usually more plastic than primary clays such as kaolin.

Setting   *See* Placing.

Sgraffito   Literally 'scratched through', by cutting or carving, a design through a coating of slip to reveal the colour of the body beneath. Carried out at the leatherhard stage.

Shrinkage   Amount by which a ceramic object is reduced in size due to drying out and firing.

Sieve   *See* Lawn.

Slip   Clay suspended in water. Used as potter's glue. Can be coloured with oxides and used for decoration.

Slurry   As above but not sieved or prepared. Can be used for joining.

Soak   A steady firing where heat penetrates the wares but temperature generally does not increase.

Spurs   Triangular clay supports for placing glazed wares.

Stains   A metal oxide or combination of oxides plus flint, alumina and a fluxing compound used to colour bodies and glazes.

Stoneware   Usually grey clay with refractory additions, fired to vitrification. Non-porous so suited for oven-to-table ware. Subdued colour characteristics.

Tenmoku   A lustrous brown-black stoneware glaze which breaks where thin to a red-brown.

Terracotta   Low fired unglazed red-brown ware.

Thermal shock   Sudden heating or cooling of a pot.

Thermocouple   An integral part of the pyrometer circuit which projects into the kiln to measure temperature.

Throw   To form cylindrical pots on a wheel.

Trailing   Coloured slips squeezed from rubber or plastic containers via nozzles to decorate leatherhard pots.

Turning   Finishing the feet of pots thrown on a wheel, by paring and shaving away excess thickness.

Underglaze decoration   Applied to biscuit prior to glazing. Restricted colour possibilities depending on glaze maturation temperature.

Vitrify   A clay body fuses during firing to become non-porous.

Ware   Ceramic artefacts, either green, biscuit or glaze fired.

Warping   Due to uneven heating and shrinkage either during drying or firing.

Water   In clay. Free water escapes when clay dries. Chemically combined water is driven off during firing between 350° centigrade and 700° centigrade.

Wax resist   Melted wax or proprietory brands can be painted on to a pot to resist adhesion of slips, glazes or pigments as a means of decoration.

Weathering   Clay exposed to the elements becomes more plastic.

Wedging   Process of mixing clay vigorously, by cutting and slamming, to exclude air and homogenise.

Whirler   Small, hand-turned wheel, used for decoration.

Further Reading

Below is just a selection of the many books available on the subject.

Cooper, Emmanuel, *A History of World Pottery* (B. T. Batsford 1972)

Gibson, John, *Pottery Decoration* (Black 1987)

Green, David, *Pottery: Materials and Techniques* (Faber and Faber 1987)

Lane, Peter, *Studio Porcelain* (Pitman House 1980)

Leach, Bernard, *A Potter's Book* (Faber and Faber 1939)

Lynggaard, Finn, *Pottery: Raku Techniques* (Van Nostrand Reinhold Company 1973)

Rhodes, Daniel, *Clay and Glazes for the Potter* (Chilton Book Company 1967)

Rhodes, Daniel, *Stoneware and Porcelain* (Pitman Publishing 1960)

Ruscoe, William, *A Manual for the Potter* (Tiranti 1959)

Sanders, N. K., *Prehistoric Art in Europe* (Penguin 1985)

Savage, George, *Pottery Through the Ages* (Pelican 1959)

Shafer, Thomas, *Pottery Decoration* (Watson-Guptill Publications 1976)

Useful Addresses

POTTERY SUPPLIES

Acme Marls Ltd
Bourne Bank
Burslem
Stoke-on-Trent
ST6 3DW
(01782 577757)

W. G. Ball Limited
Longton Mill
Anchor Road
Longton
Stoke-on-Trent
ST3 1JW
(01782 313956/312286)

Cromartie Kilns Ltd
Park Hall Road
Longton
Stoke-on-Trent
ST3 5AY
(01782 313947)

Fordham Thermal Systems Co. Ltd
Studlands Park Industrial Estate
Newmarket
Suffolk
CB8 7EA
(01638 666020)

Moira Pottery Company Ltd
Moira
Burton-on-Trent
Staffordshire
DE12 6DF
(01283 221961)

Potclays
Brickkiln Lane
Etruria
Stoke-on-Trent
ST4 7BP
(01782 219816)

Potterycrafts Limited
Campbell Road
Stoke-on-Trent
ST4 4ET
(01782 272444)

Valentine Clay Products
The Shiphouse
Birches Head Road
Hanley
Stoke-on-Trent
ST1 6LH
(01782 271200)

GENERAL INFORMATION

Craftsmen Potters Association of
Great Britain
William Blake House
Marshall Street
London
W1V 1FD
(0171 437 7605)

Crafts Council
12 Waterloo Place
London
SW1 4AU
(0171 930 4811)

Index

Kiln
  firing 146–51
  furniture 27, 143–5
  packing 140–6
  shelves 143
  sitter 53
Kilns 37–8
  downdraught 45
  electric 44, 50, 52, 147
  gas 47–50, 149–51
  updraught 45
  wood 46–7

Leatherhard 65
Limestone 159
  cave 167
Lustres 155, 178

Magnesium oxide 161
Manganese dioxide 177
Metal oxides 161–2
Metamorphosis 13, 44, 139
Molecular structure 13
Monkey-face spiral 22
Mould making 74–9

Oxides
  common 168
  decoration 24, 153
Ox-head spiral 22

Palaeolithic 5, 6
Particles, clay 10, 15
Pinch pots 63–5
Plaster of Paris 16, 74–7, 79, 120
Plasticity 5, 10, 19
Porcelain 8, 139, 156
Porous/porosity 5, 6
Potter's wheel 8, 36, 38, 40–3
Preparation 17, 18, 103
Press dish 16, 70–1
Proportion 32, 34
Pyrometer 150

Quartz 159

Raku 152–4
Reclaim 5, 13, 14, 16, 18, 24
Reconstituted 5
Recycled 15
Red earthenware 11
Refractory 12, 139
Rhodes, Daniel 159
Ritualistic 5, 6, 165
Rolling pin 59, 67, 99

'Safefire' units 53
Sand 12, 24
School 50, 146
  kilns 52–3
Scoring 65
Scraping 89
Sgraffito 173–5
Shelving 37
Shrinkage 12, 26, 34, 86
Silica 120, 158
Slab 6
Slabbing 65–89
Slip 65, 169
  casting 74–8
  decoration 169–72
  recipes 179
Slipware, English 157
Slurry 15
Soaking down 14, 15
Stoneware 13, 139, 156
Stress 27
Suppliers, pottery 12

Temperature control 52–3
Terracotta 11, 139
Texture 166–7
Thermocouple 145
Throwing 102–31
  bowls/lids 129
  cylinders 112–3
  plates 131
  vases 120
Toft brothers 171
Tongs 153
Tools 55–61
Turning 133–7
  tools 57

Vitrify 13, 138, 155, 156

Wheel 8, 36, 38
  thrown 26
  head 43, 120
Wheels
  kick/momentum 40–1
  power 41–3
  second-hand 42
Wheelwork 101–32
  preparation 103
  tools 103
Woodash 159
  washing 160
Workshop 36–9

Zinc oxide 161

6722